KWEZI™

COLLECTOR'S EDITION
ISSUE: 13 - 15

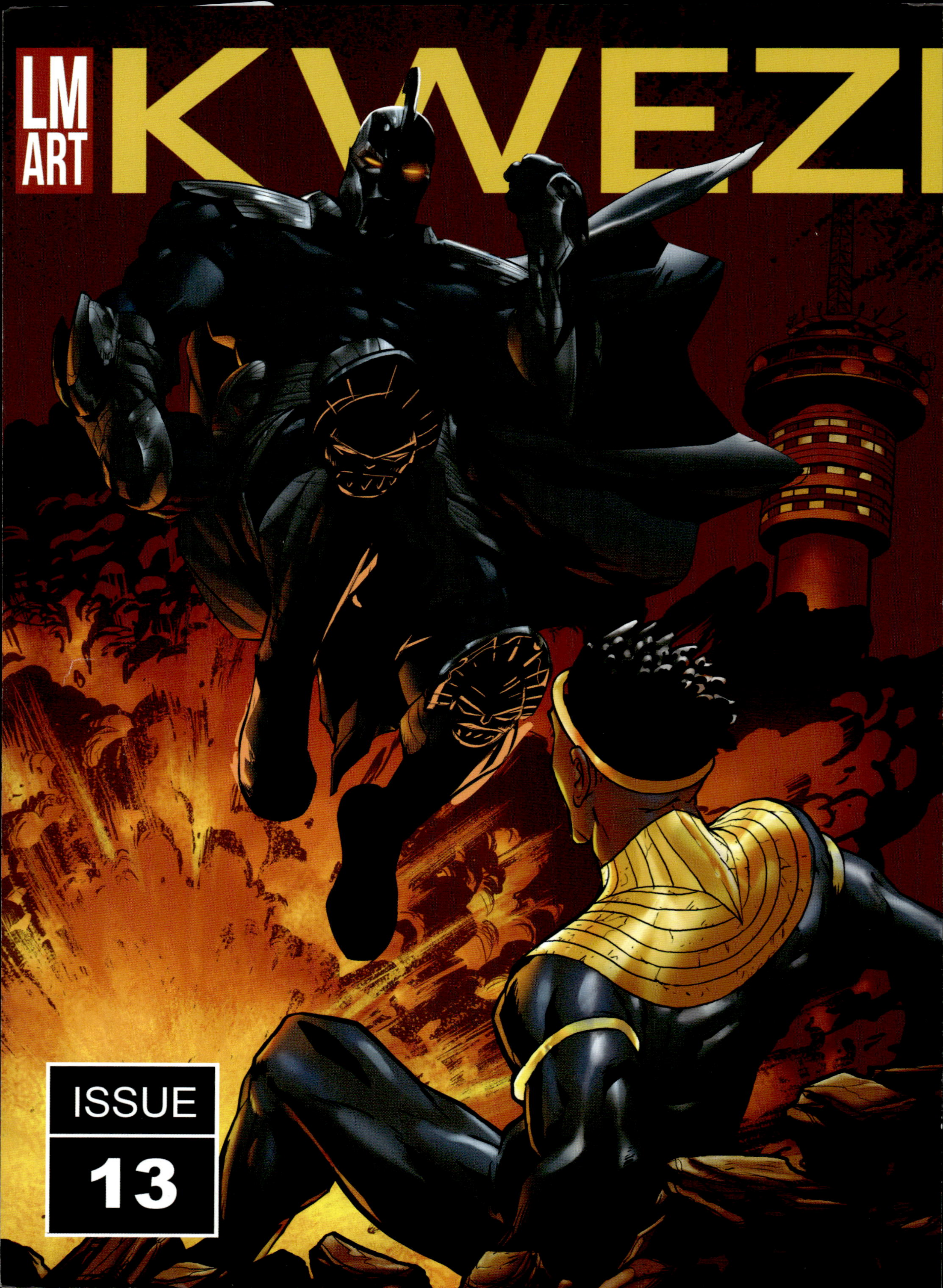
LM
ART
KWEZI
ISSUE
13

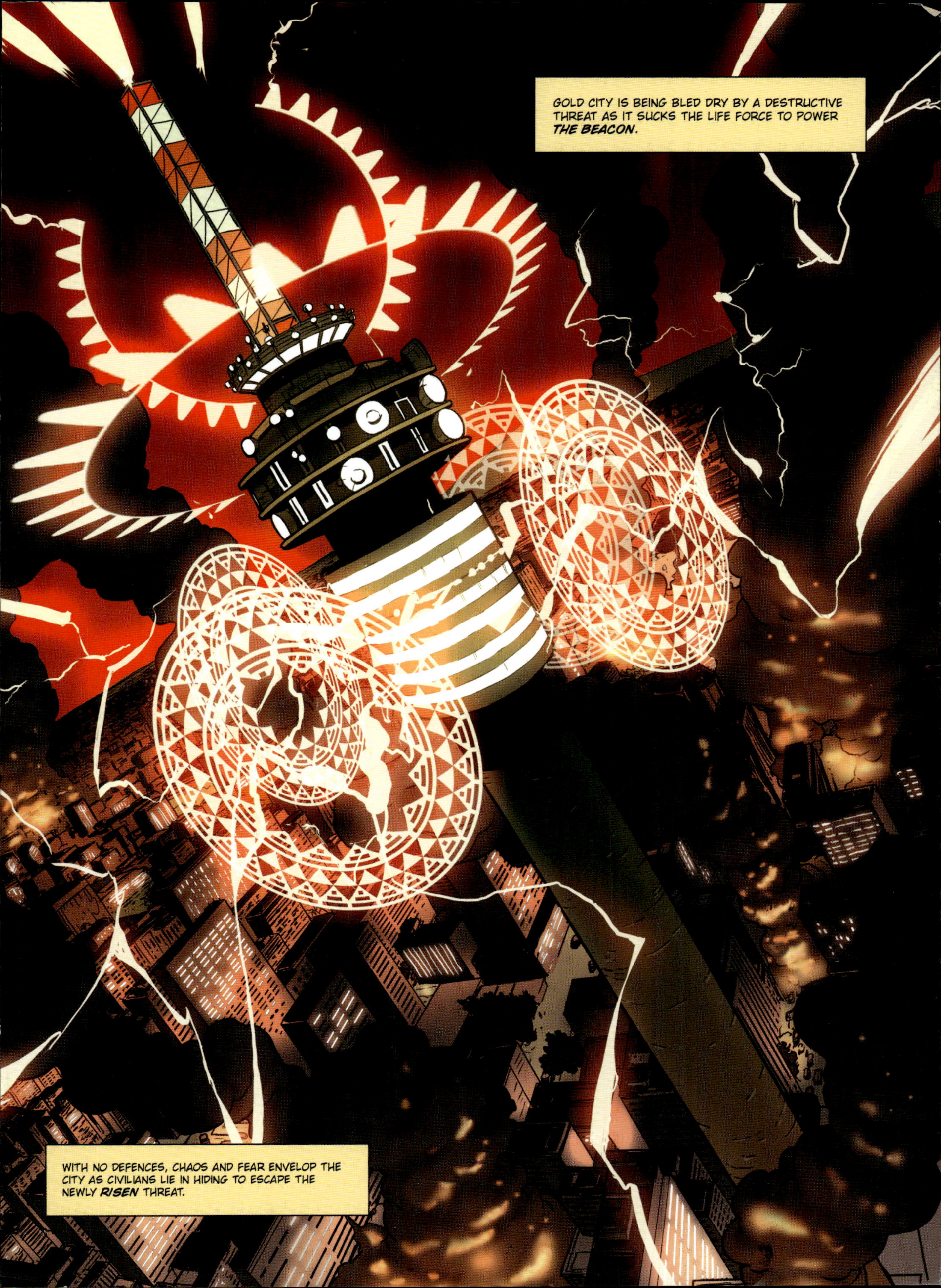
GOLD CITY IS BEING BLED DRY BY A DESTRUCTIVE THREAT AS IT SUCKS THE LIFE FORCE TO POWER *THE BEACON*.
WITH NO DEFENCES, CHAOS AND FEAR ENVELOP THE CITY AS CIVILIANS LIE IN HIDING TO ESCAPE THE NEWLY *RISEN* THREAT.

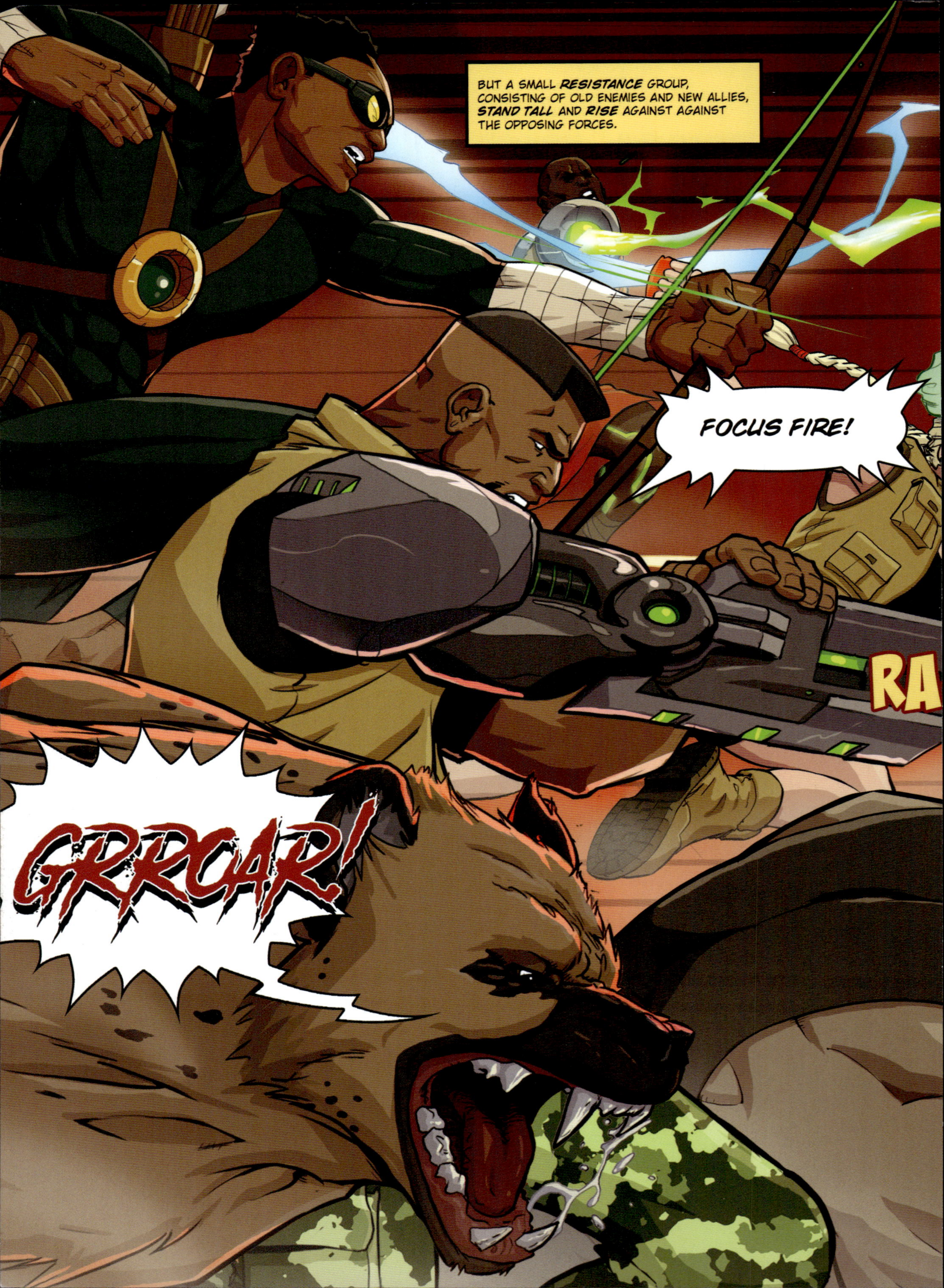
BUT A SMALL RESISTANCE GROUP, CONSISTING OF OLD ENEMIES AND NEW ALLIES, STAND TALL AND RISE AGAINST AGAINST THE OPPOSING FORCES.
FOCUS FIRE!
RA
GRRROAR!

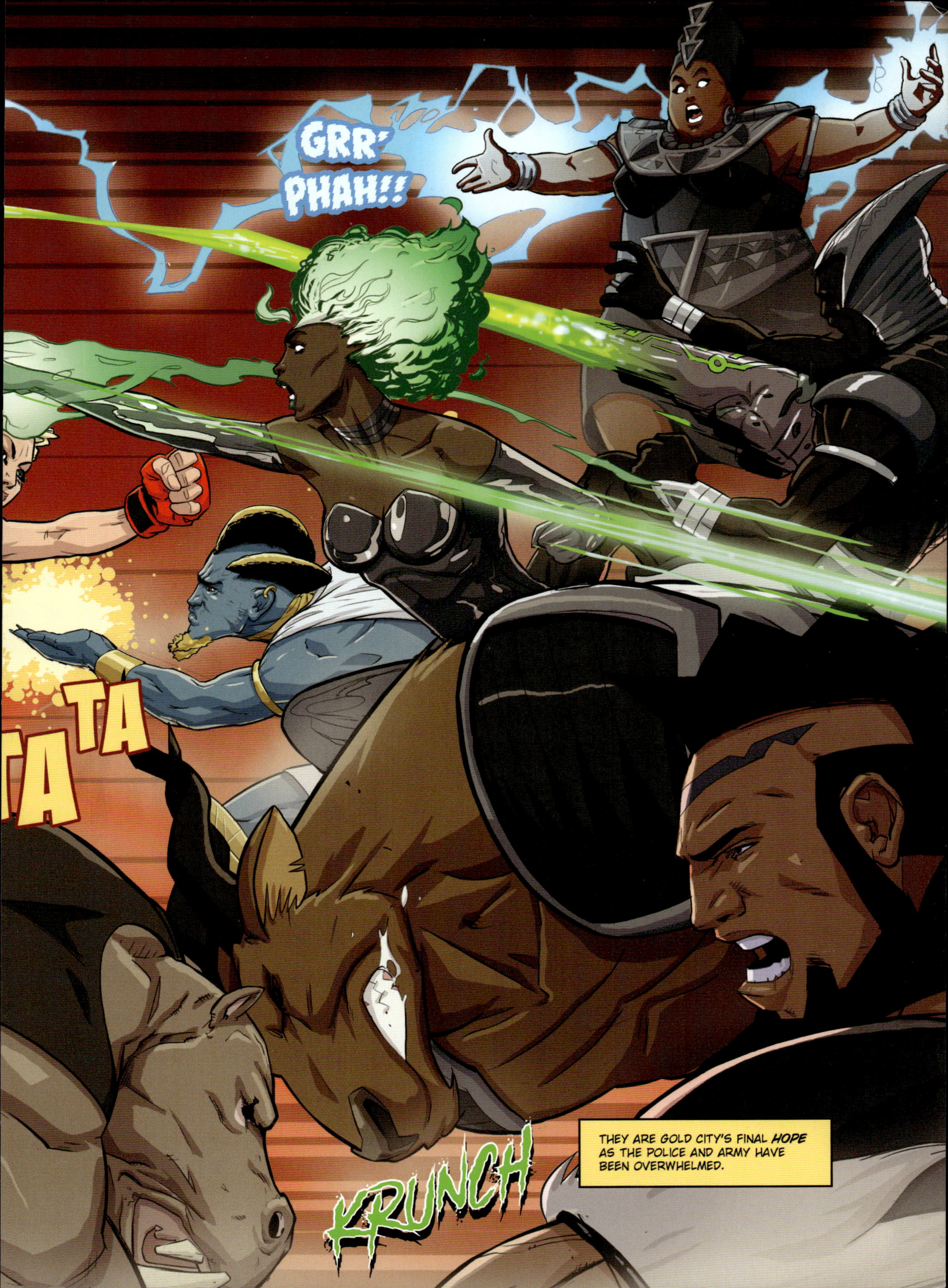
GRR' PHAH!!
TA TA
THEY ARE GOLD CITY'S FINAL *HOPE* AS THE POLICE AND ARMY HAVE BEEN OVERWHELMED.
KRUNCH

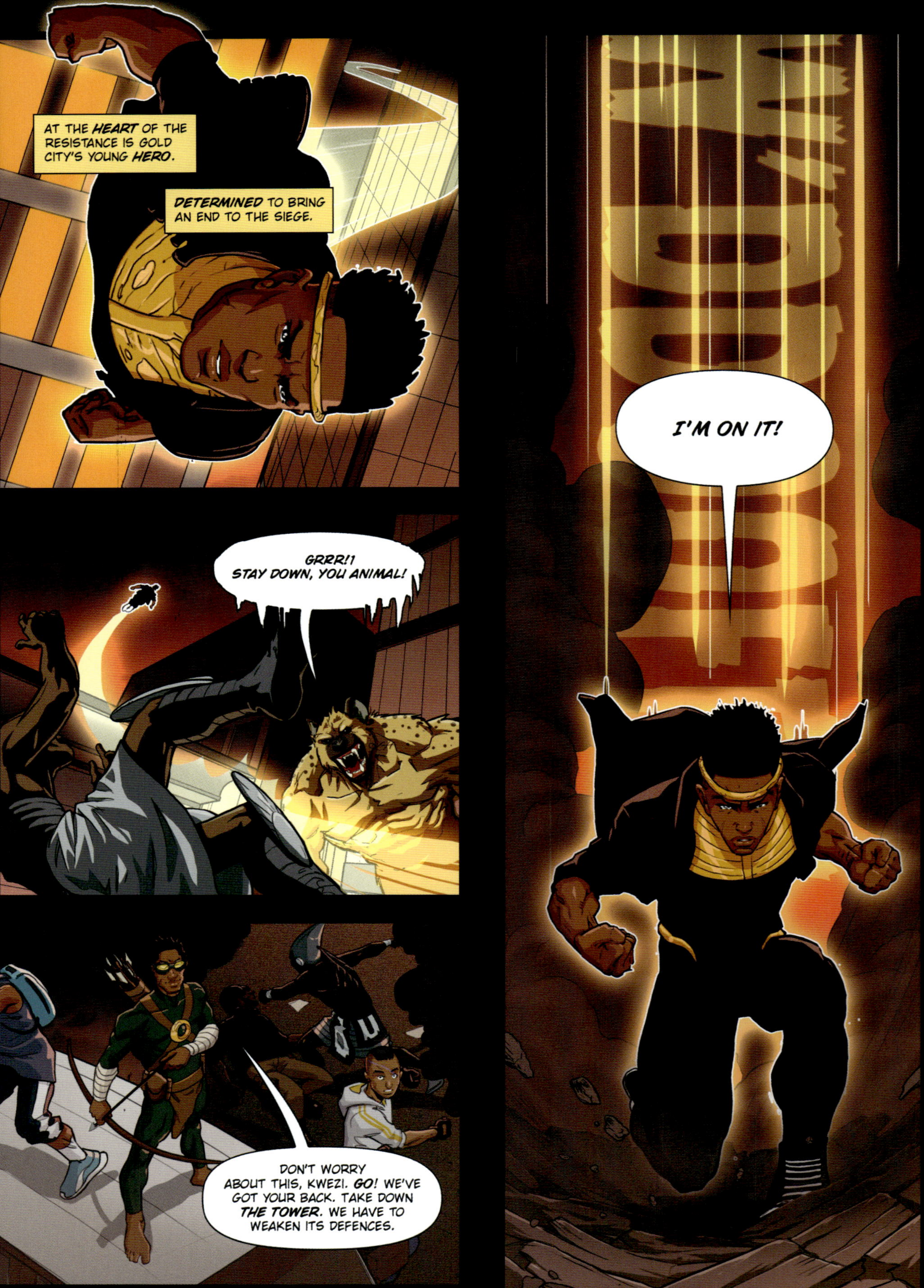
AT THE *HEART* OF THE RESISTANCE IS GOLD CITY'S YOUNG *HERO*.
DETERMINED TO BRING AN END TO THE SIEGE.
GRRR!1 STAY DOWN, YOU ANIMAL!
DON'T WORRY ABOUT THIS, KWEZI. *GO!* WE'VE GOT YOUR BACK. TAKE DOWN *THE TOWER*. WE HAVE TO WEAKEN ITS DEFENCES.
I'M ON IT!

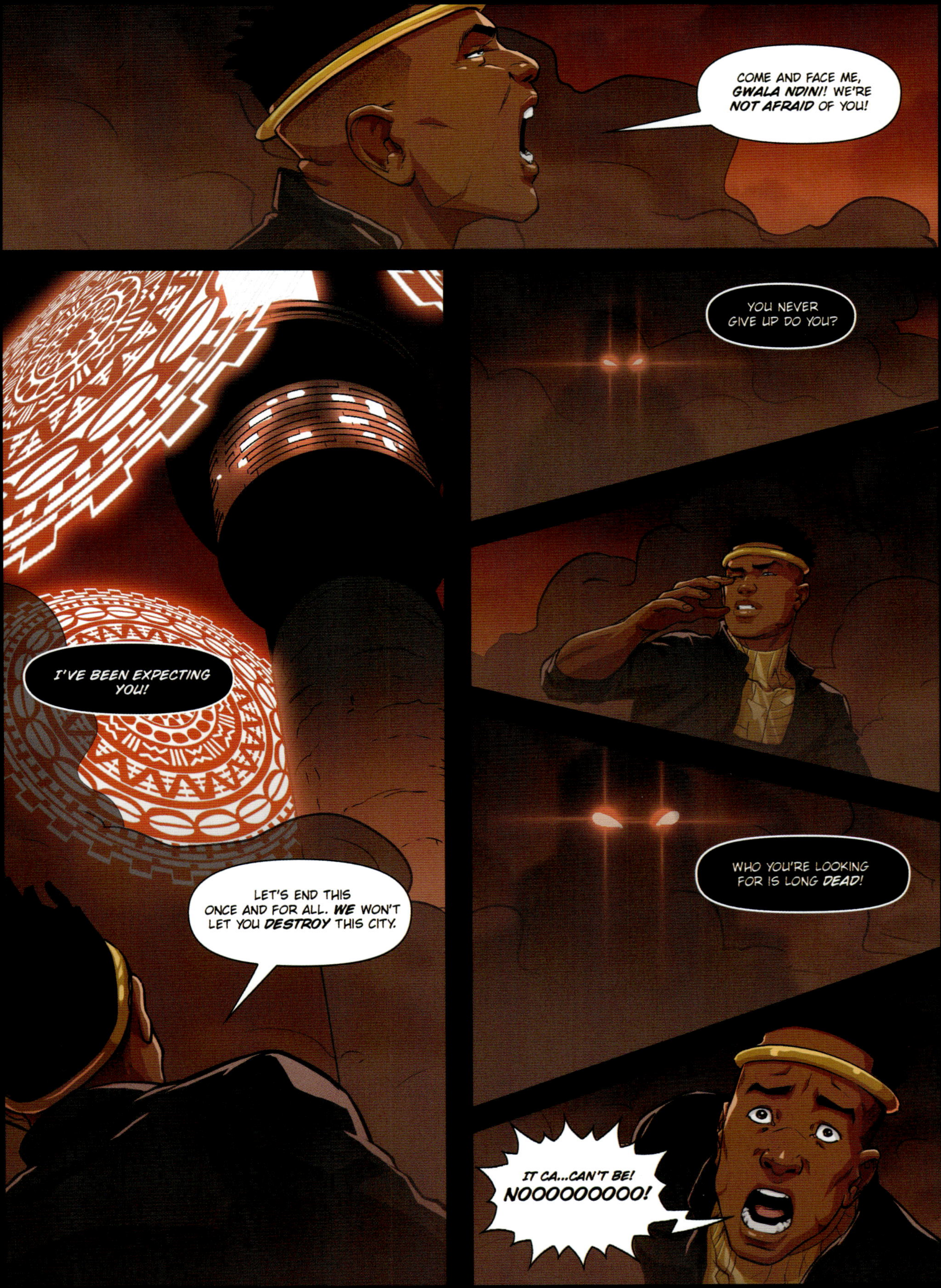
COME AND FACE ME, GWALA NDINI! WE'RE NOT AFRAID OF YOU!
I'VE BEEN EXPECTING YOU!
LET'S END THIS ONCE AND FOR ALL. WE WON'T LET YOU DESTROY THIS CITY.
YOU NEVER GIVE UP DO YOU?
WHO YOU'RE LOOKING FOR IS LONG DEAD!
IT CA...CAN'T BE! NOOOOOOOOO!

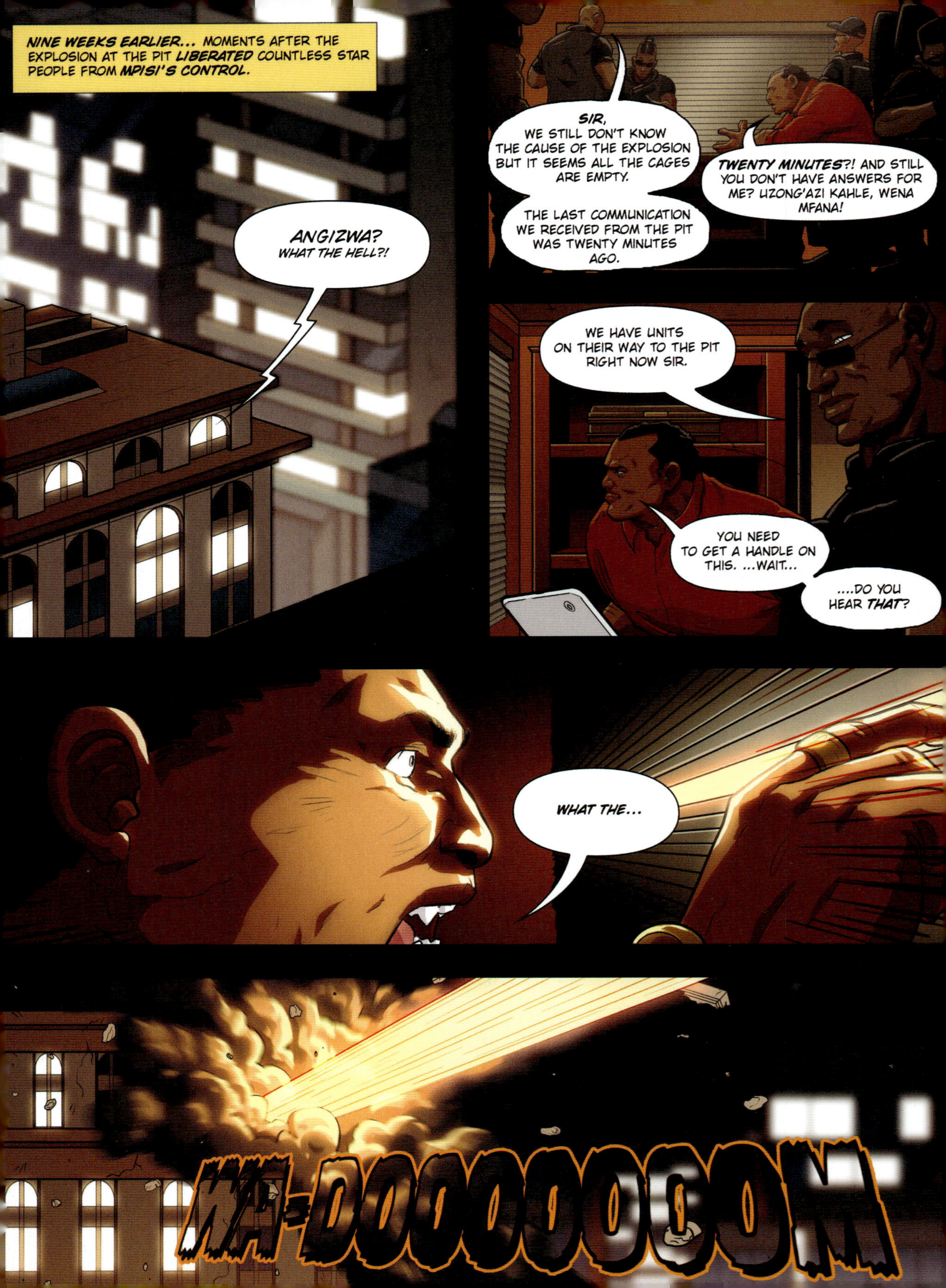
NINE WEEKS EARLIER... MOMENTS AFTER THE EXPLOSION AT THE PIT LIBERATED COUNTLESS STAR PEOPLE FROM MPISI'S CONTROL.
ANGIZWA? WHAT THE HELL?!
SIR, WE STILL DON'T KNOW THE CAUSE OF THE EXPLOSION BUT IT SEEMS ALL THE CAGES ARE EMPTY.
THE LAST COMMUNICATION WE RECEIVED FROM THE PIT WAS TWENTY MINUTES AGO.
TWENTY MINUTES?! AND STILL YOU DON'T HAVE ANSWERS FOR ME? UZONG'AZI KAHLE, WENA MFANA!
WE HAVE UNITS ON THEIR WAY TO THE PIT RIGHT NOW SIR.
YOU NEED TO GET A HANDLE ON THIS. ...WAIT...
....DO YOU HEAR THAT?
WHAT THE...
KA-DOOOOOOOOM

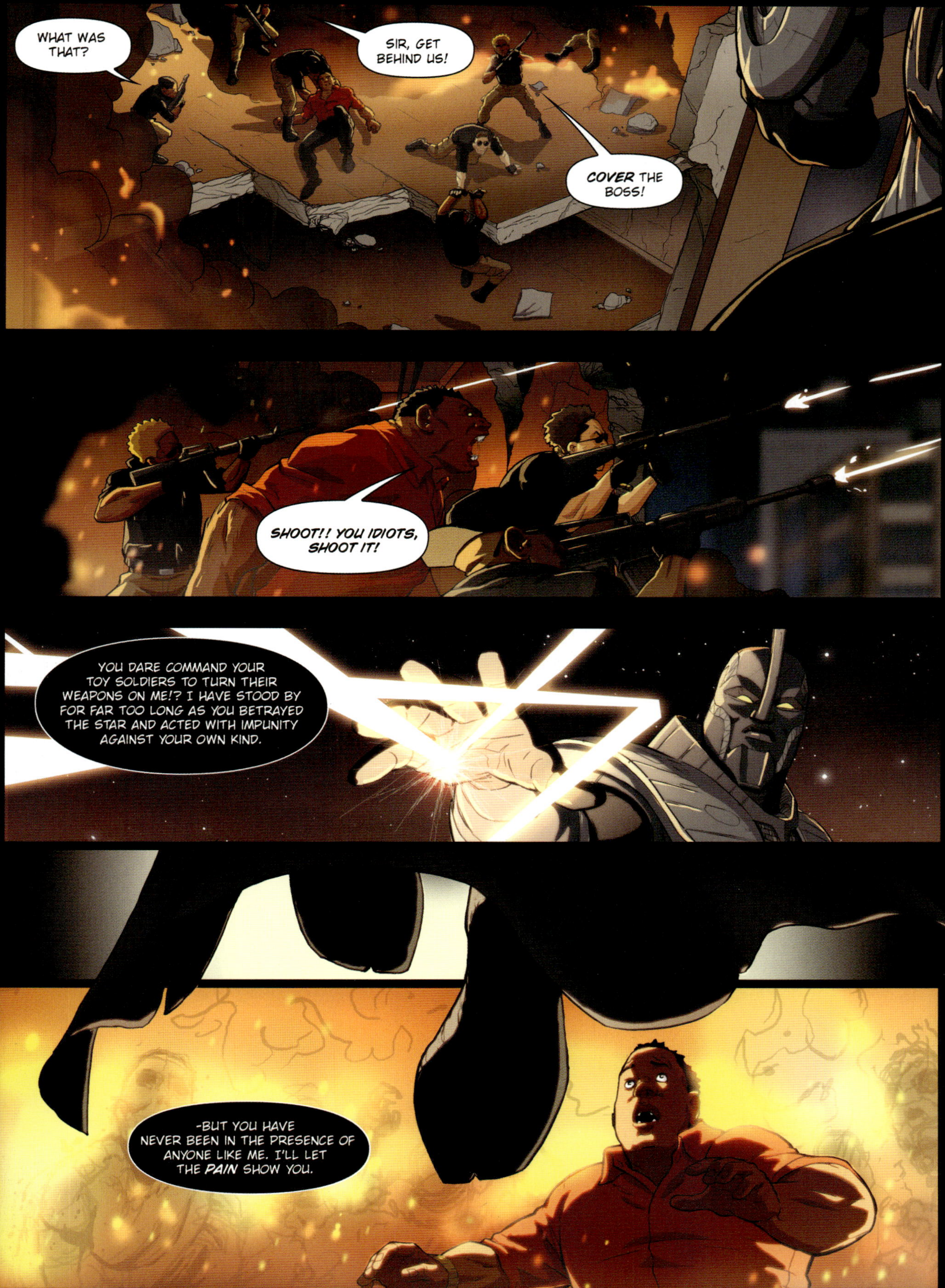
WHAT WAS THAT?
SIR, GET BEHIND US!
COVER THE BOSS!
SHOOT!! YOU IDIOTS, SHOOT IT!
YOU DARE COMMAND YOUR TOY SOLDIERS TO TURN THEIR WEAPONS ON ME!? I HAVE STOOD BY FOR FAR TOO LONG AS YOU BETRAYED THE STAR AND ACTED WITH IMPUNITY AGAINST YOUR OWN KIND.
-BUT YOU HAVE NEVER BEEN IN THE PRESENCE OF ANYONE LIKE ME. I'LL LET THE PAIN SHOW YOU.

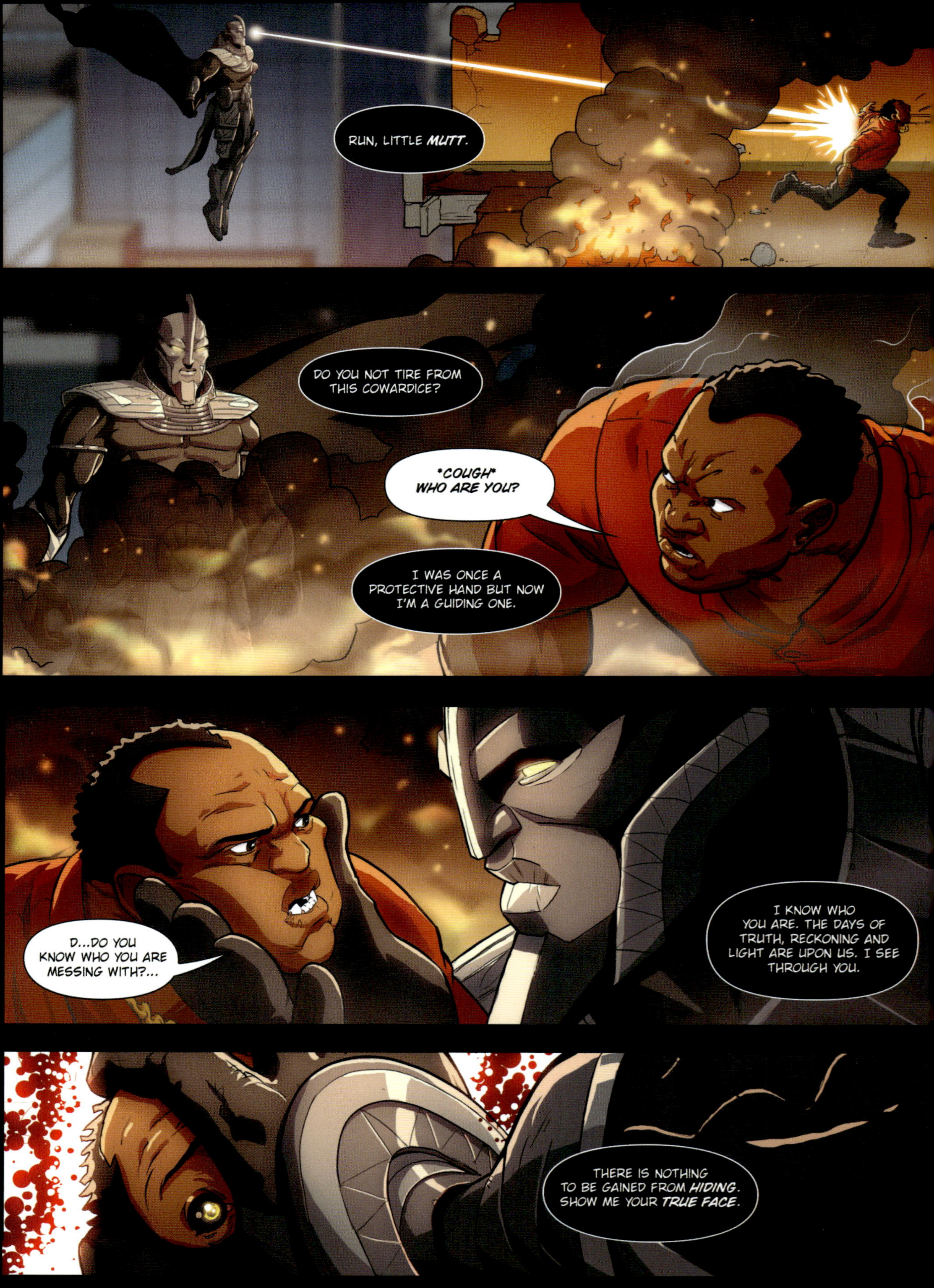
RUN, LITTLE MUTT.
DO YOU NOT TIRE FROM THIS COWARDICE?
COUGH WHO ARE YOU?
I WAS ONCE A PROTECTIVE HAND BUT NOW I'M A GUIDING ONE.
D...DO YOU KNOW WHO YOU ARE MESSING WITH?...
I KNOW WHO YOU ARE. THE DAYS OF TRUTH, RECKONING AND LIGHT ARE UPON US. I SEE THROUGH YOU.
THERE IS NOTHING TO BE GAINED FROM HIDING. SHOW ME YOUR TRUE FACE.

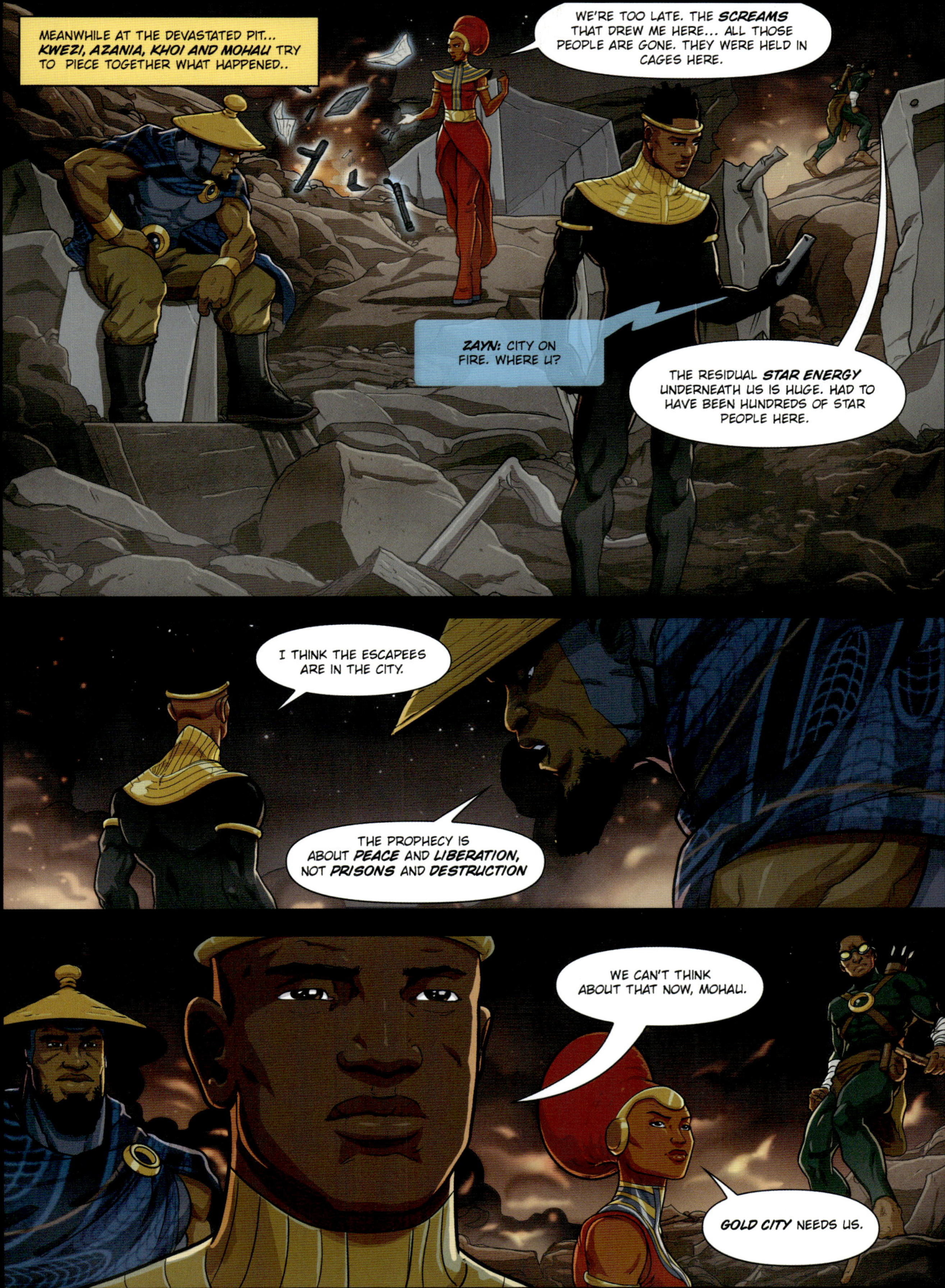

MEANWHILE AT THE DEVASTATED PIT... **KWEZI, AZANIA, KHOI AND MOHAU** TRY TO PIECE TOGETHER WHAT HAPPENED..
WE'RE TOO LATE. THE **SCREAMS** THAT DREW ME HERE... ALL THOSE PEOPLE ARE GONE. THEY WERE HELD IN CAGES HERE.
ZAYN: CITY ON FIRE. WHERE U?
THE RESIDUAL **STAR ENERGY** UNDERNEATH US IS HUGE. HAD TO HAVE BEEN HUNDREDS OF STAR PEOPLE HERE.
I THINK THE ESCAPEES ARE IN THE CITY.
THE PROPHECY IS ABOUT **PEACE** AND **LIBERATION,** NOT **PRISONS** AND **DESTRUCTION**
WE CAN'T THINK ABOUT THAT NOW, MOHAU.
GOLD CITY NEEDS US.

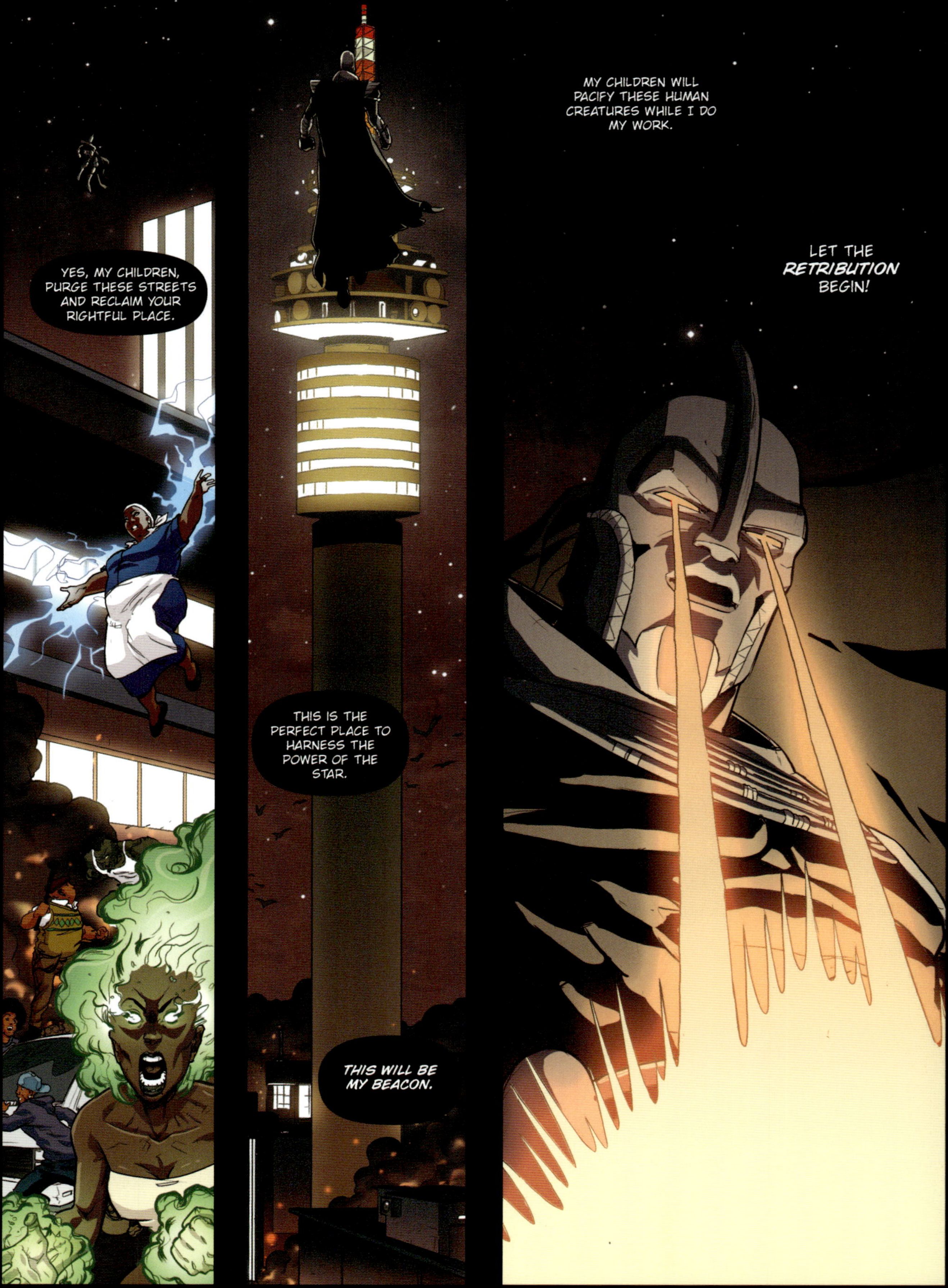
YES, MY CHILDREN, PURGE THESE STREETS AND RECLAIM YOUR RIGHTFUL PLACE.
THIS IS THE PERFECT PLACE TO HARNESS THE POWER OF THE STAR.
THIS WILL BE MY BEACON.
MY CHILDREN WILL PACIFY THESE HUMAN CREATURES WHILE I DO MY WORK.
LET THE RETRIBUTION BEGIN!

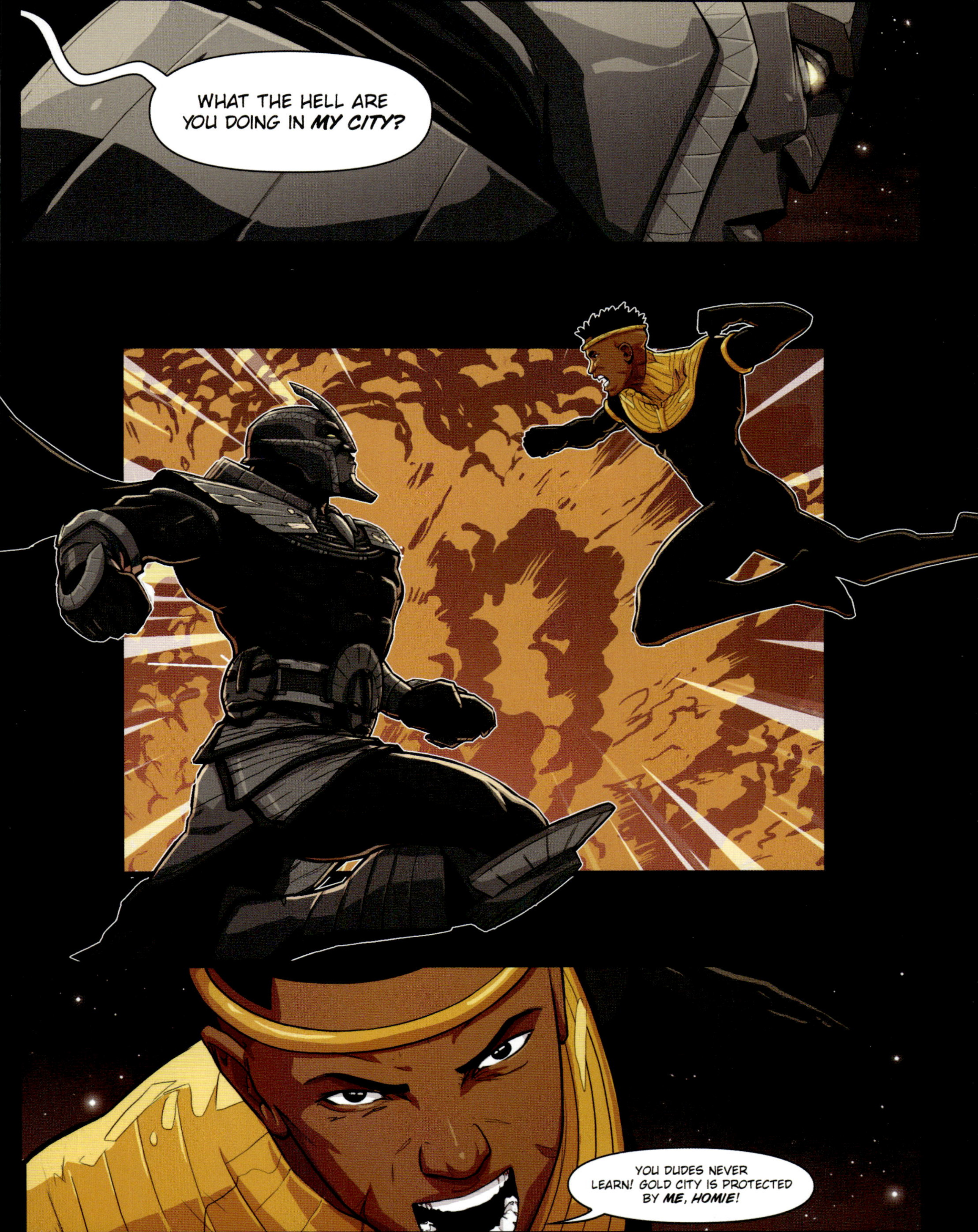
WHAT THE HELL ARE YOU DOING IN MY CITY?
YOU DUDES NEVER LEARN! GOLD CITY IS PROTECTED BY ME, HOMIE!

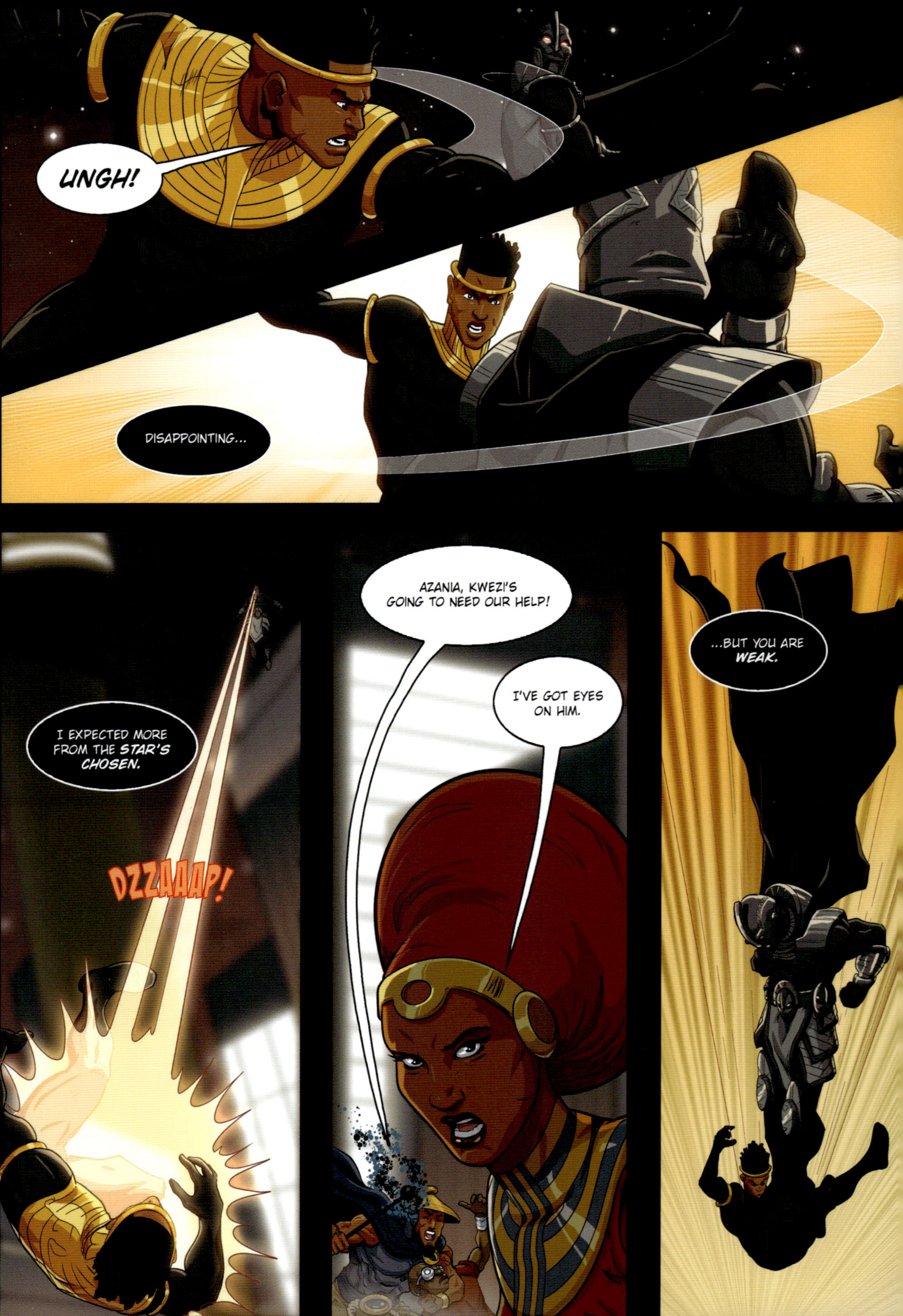
UNGH!
DISAPPOINTING...
I EXPECTED MORE FROM THE STAR'S CHOSEN.
DZZAAAP!
AZANIA, KWEZI'S GOING TO NEED OUR HELP!
I'VE GOT EYES ON HIM.
...BUT YOU ARE WEAK.

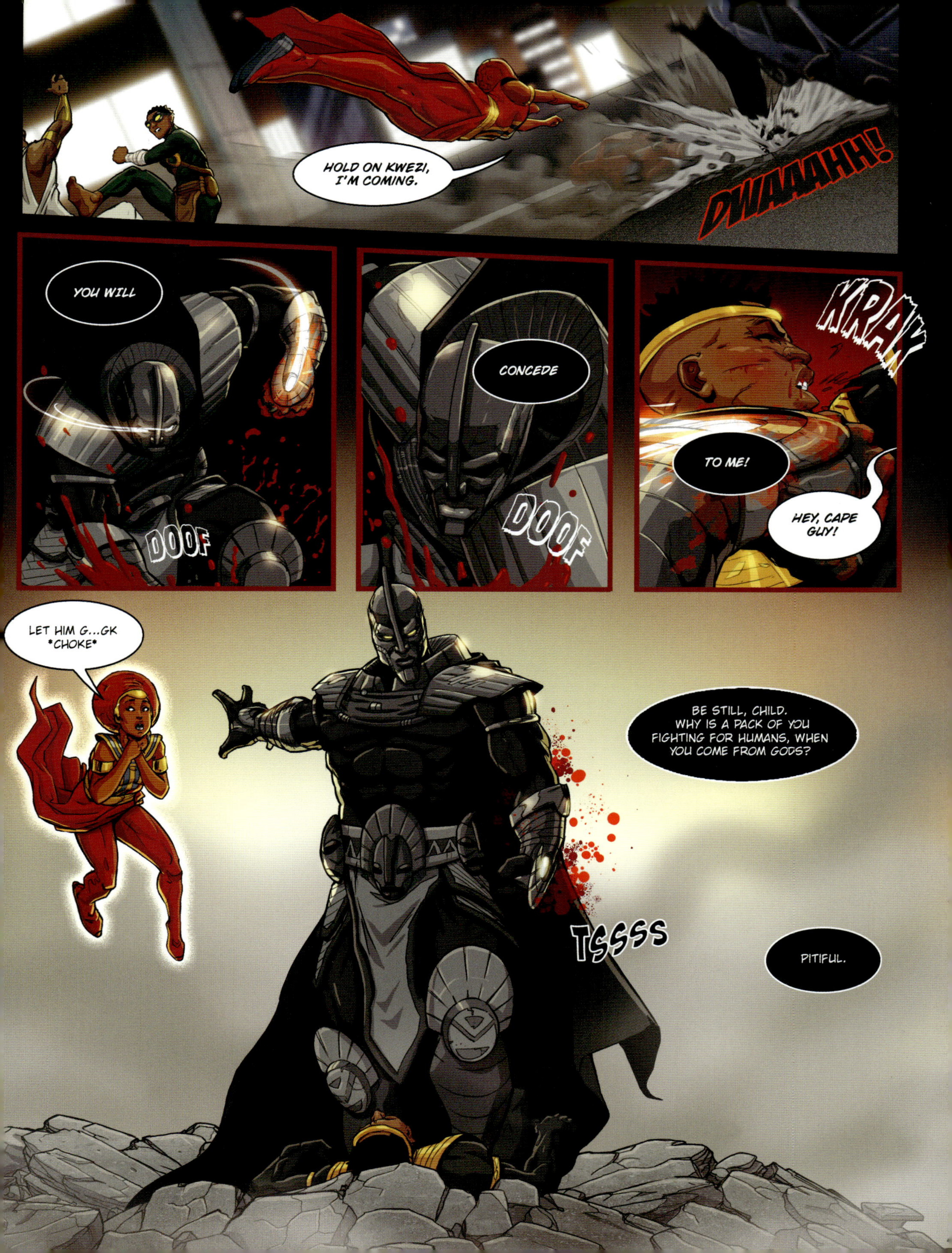
HOLD ON KWEZI, I'M COMING.
DWAAAHH!
YOU WILL
DOOF
CONCEDE
DOOF
KRAK
TO ME!
HEY, CAPE GUY!
LET HIM G...GK *CHOKE*
BE STILL, CHILD. WHY IS A PACK OF YOU FIGHTING FOR HUMANS, WHEN YOU COME FROM GODS?
TSSSS
PITIFUL.

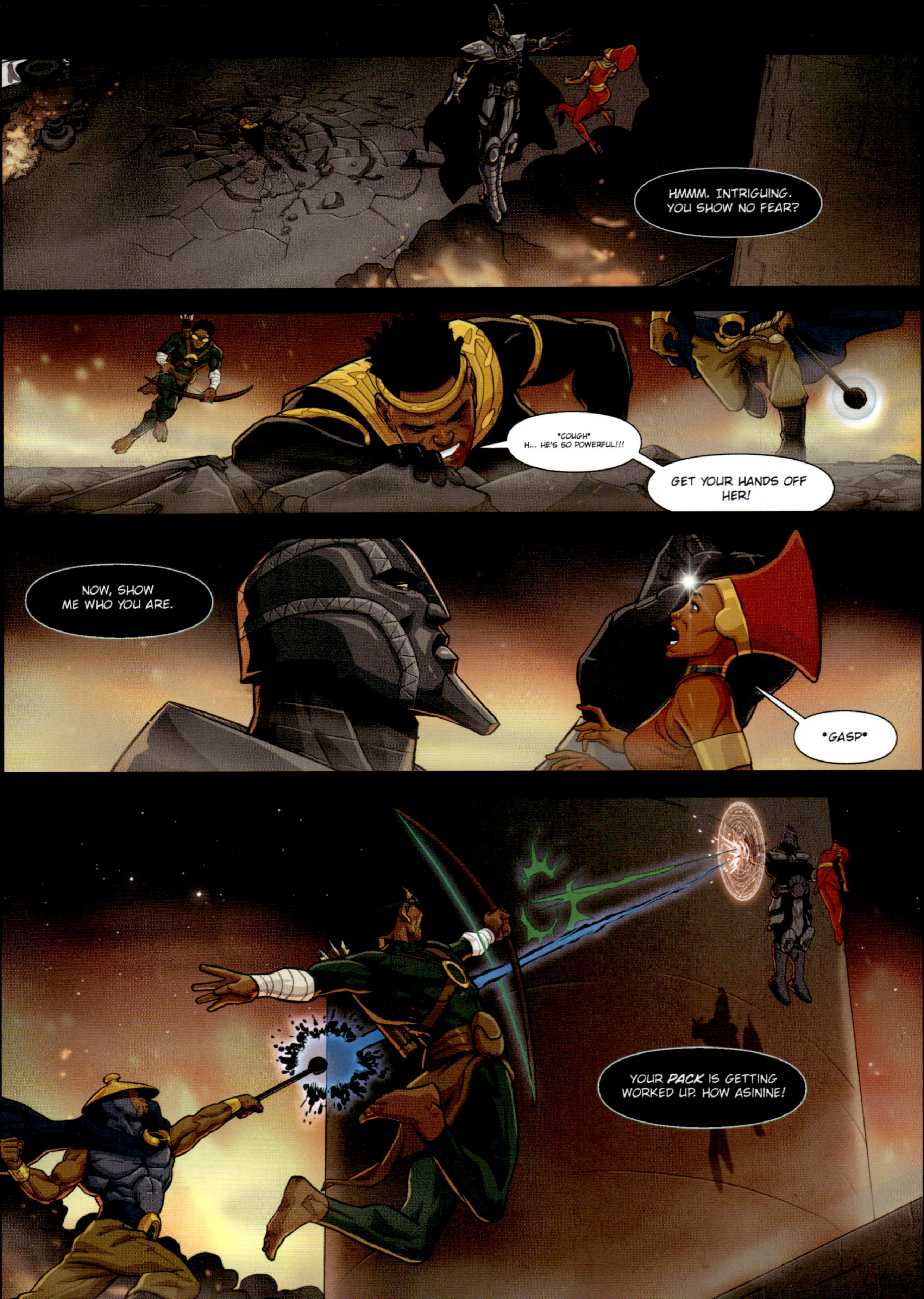
HMMM. INTRIGUING. YOU SHOW NO FEAR?
COUGH H... HE'S SO POWERFUL!!!
GET YOUR HANDS OFF HER!
NOW, SHOW ME WHO YOU ARE.
GASP
YOUR PACK IS GETTING WORKED UP. HOW ASININE!

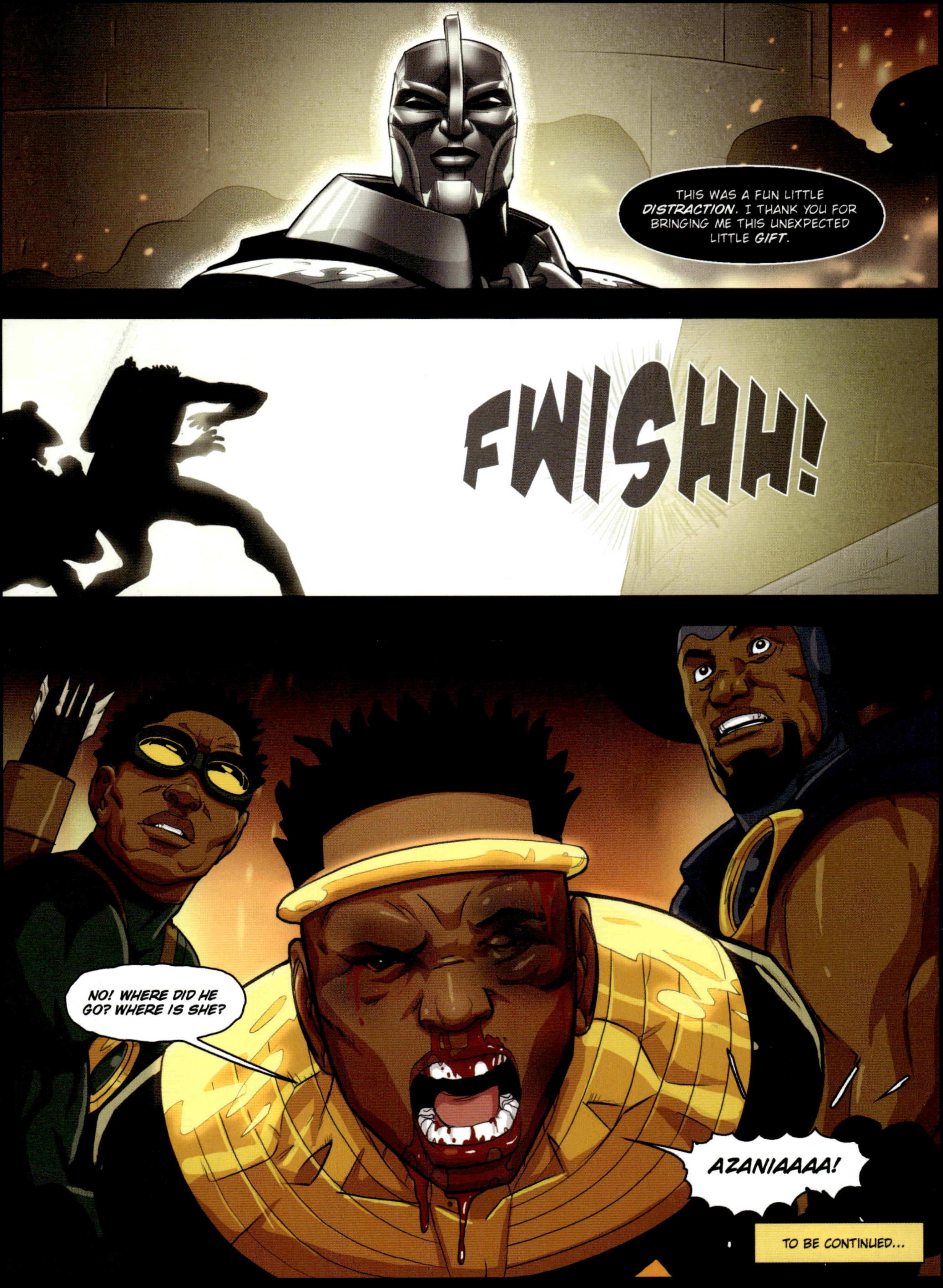
THIS WAS A FUN LITTLE DISTRACTION. I THANK YOU FOR BRINGING ME THIS UNEXPECTED LITTLE GIFT.
FWISHH!
NO! WHERE DID HE GO? WHERE IS SHE?
AZANIAAAA!
TO BE CONTINUED...

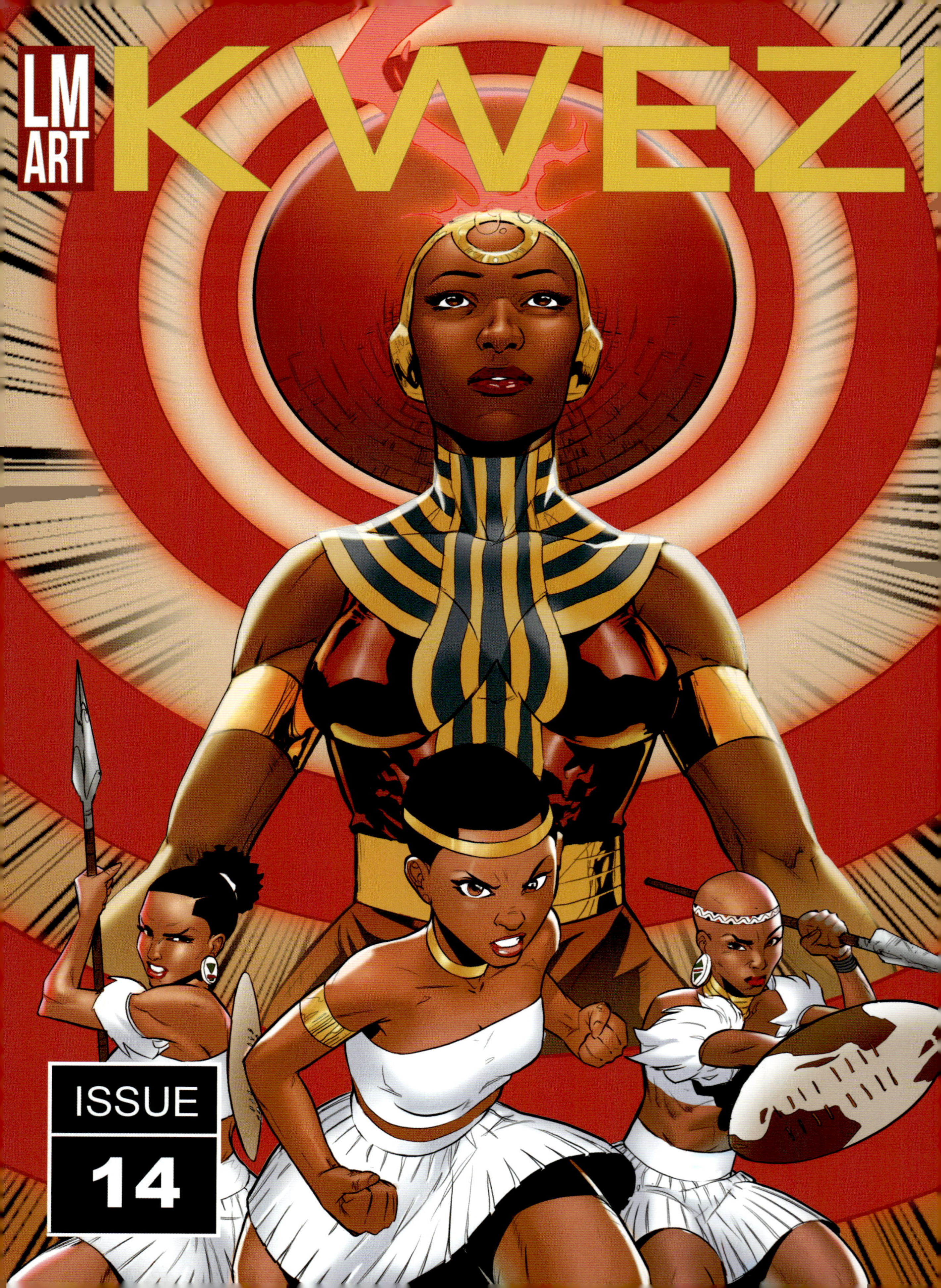
LM ART
KWEZI
ISSUE
14

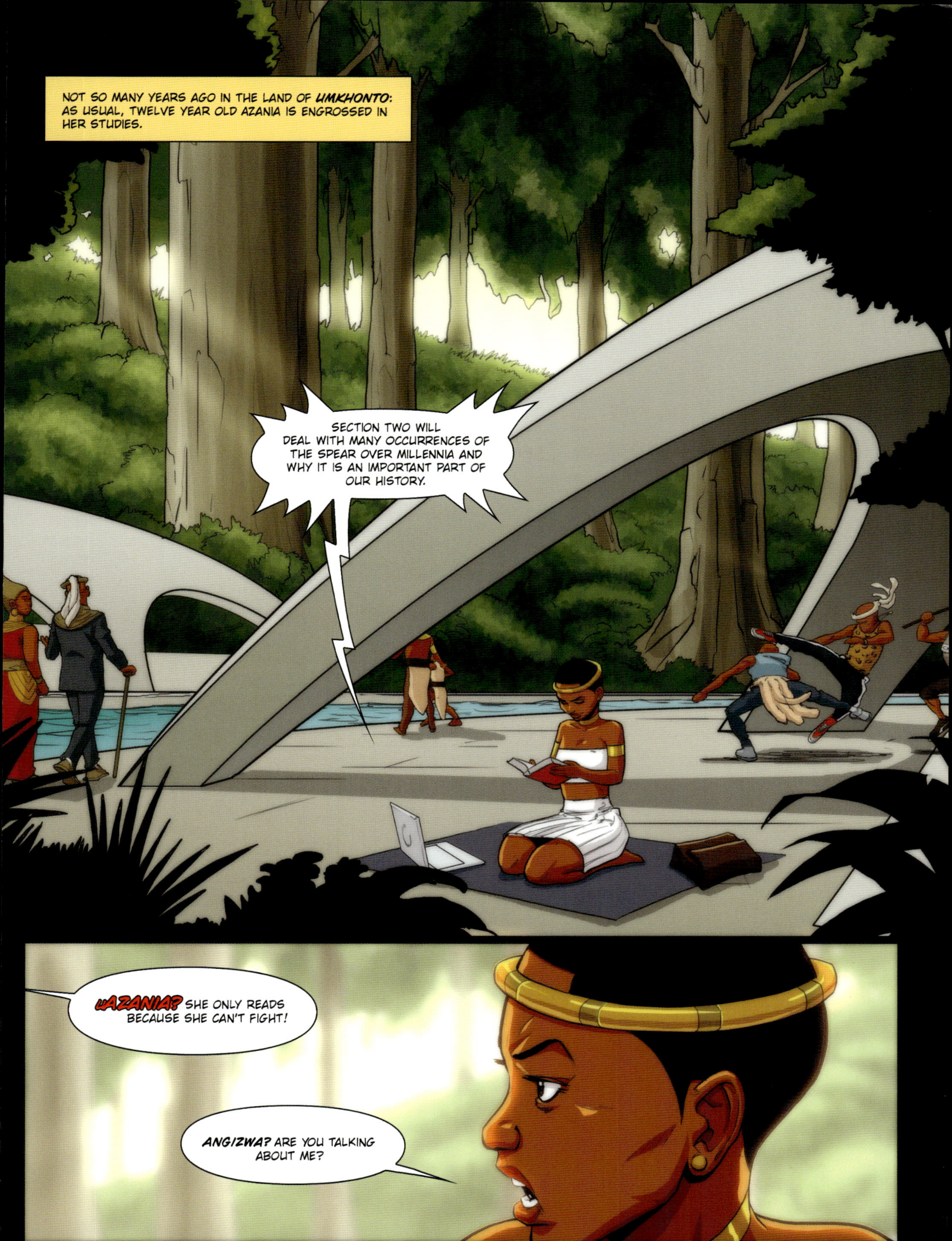
NOT SO MANY YEARS AGO IN THE LAND OF UMKHONTO: AS USUAL, TWELVE YEAR OLD AZANIA IS ENGROSSED IN HER STUDIES.
SECTION TWO WILL DEAL WITH MANY OCCURRENCES OF THE SPEAR OVER MILLENNIA AND WHY IT IS AN IMPORTANT PART OF OUR HISTORY.
uAZANIA? SHE ONLY READS BECAUSE SHE CAN'T FIGHT!
ANGIZWA? ARE YOU TALKING ABOUT ME?

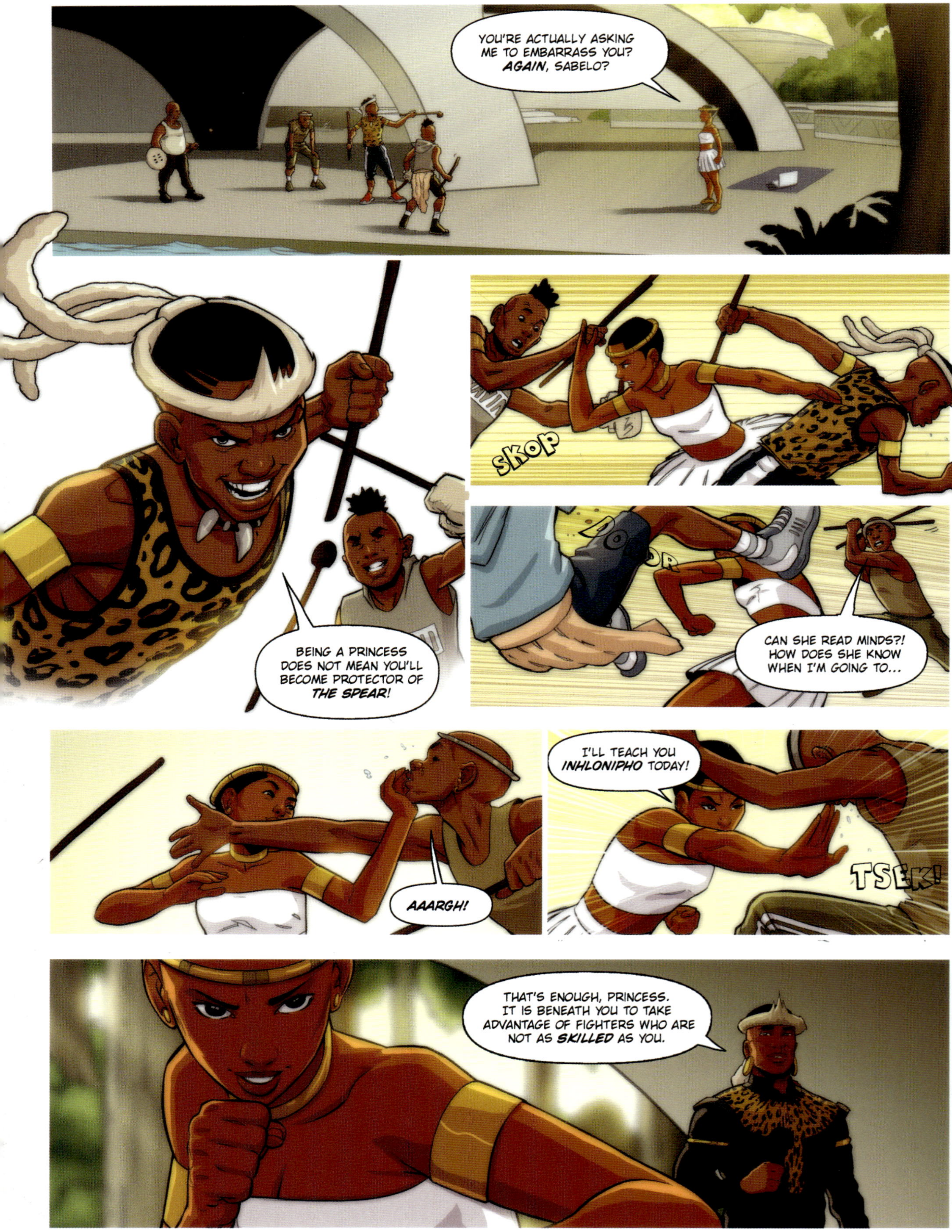

YOU'RE ACTUALLY ASKING ME TO EMBARRASS YOU? AGAIN, SABELO?
BEING A PRINCESS DOES NOT MEAN YOU'LL BECOME PROTECTOR OF THE SPEAR!
SKOP
CAN SHE READ MINDS?! HOW DOES SHE KNOW WHEN I'M GOING TO...
AAARGH!
I'LL TEACH YOU INHLONIPHO TODAY!
TSEK!
THAT'S ENOUGH, PRINCESS. IT IS BENEATH YOU TO TAKE ADVANTAGE OF FIGHTERS WHO ARE NOT AS SKILLED AS YOU.

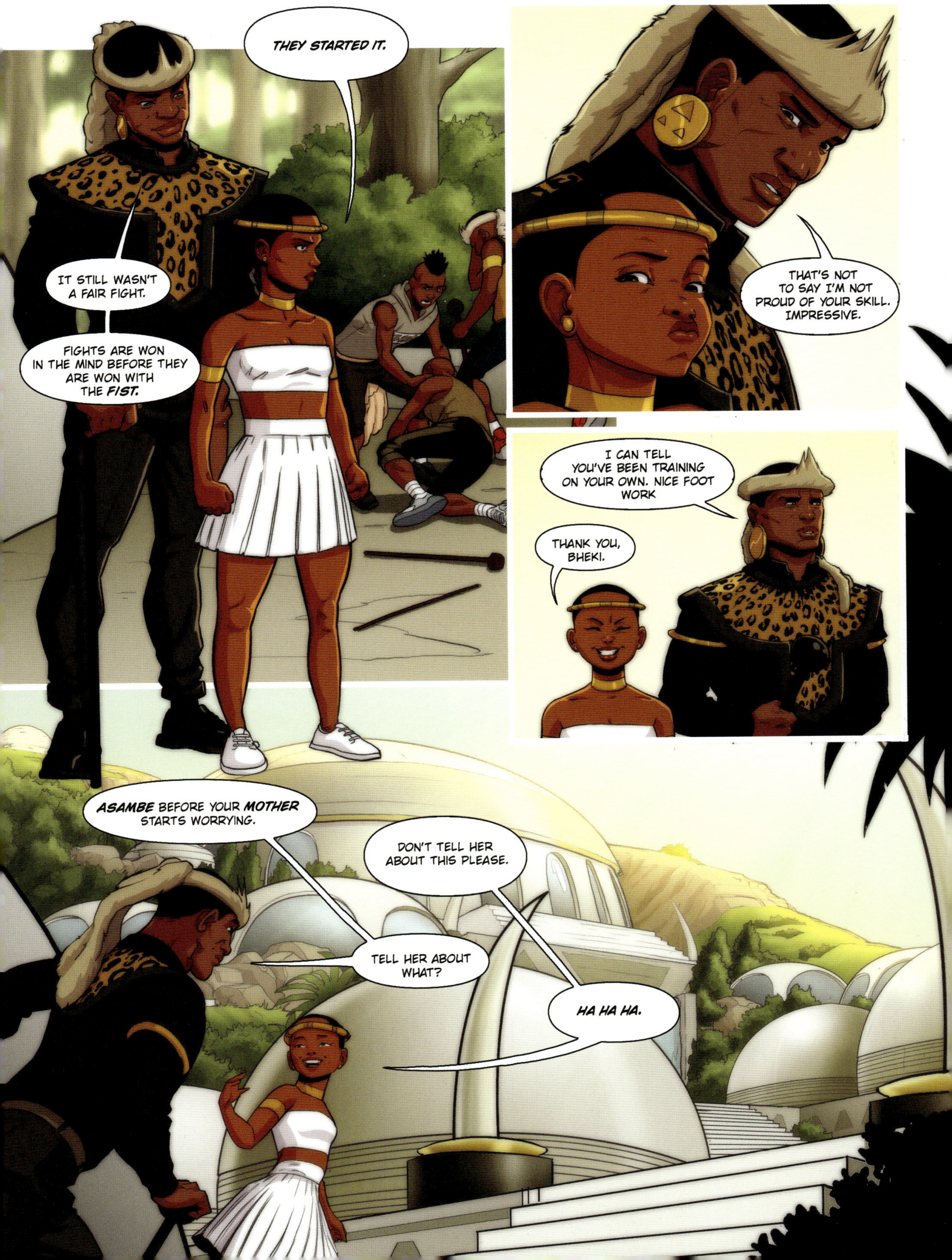
THEY STARTED IT.
IT STILL WASN'T A FAIR FIGHT.
FIGHTS ARE WON IN THE MIND BEFORE THEY ARE WON WITH THE ***FIST.***
THAT'S NOT TO SAY I'M NOT PROUD OF YOUR SKILL. IMPRESSIVE.
I CAN TELL YOU'VE BEEN TRAINING ON YOUR OWN. NICE FOOT WORK
THANK YOU, BHEKI.
ASAMBE BEFORE YOUR ***MOTHER*** STARTS WORRYING.
DON'T TELL HER ABOUT THIS PLEASE.
TELL HER ABOUT WHAT?
HA HA HA.

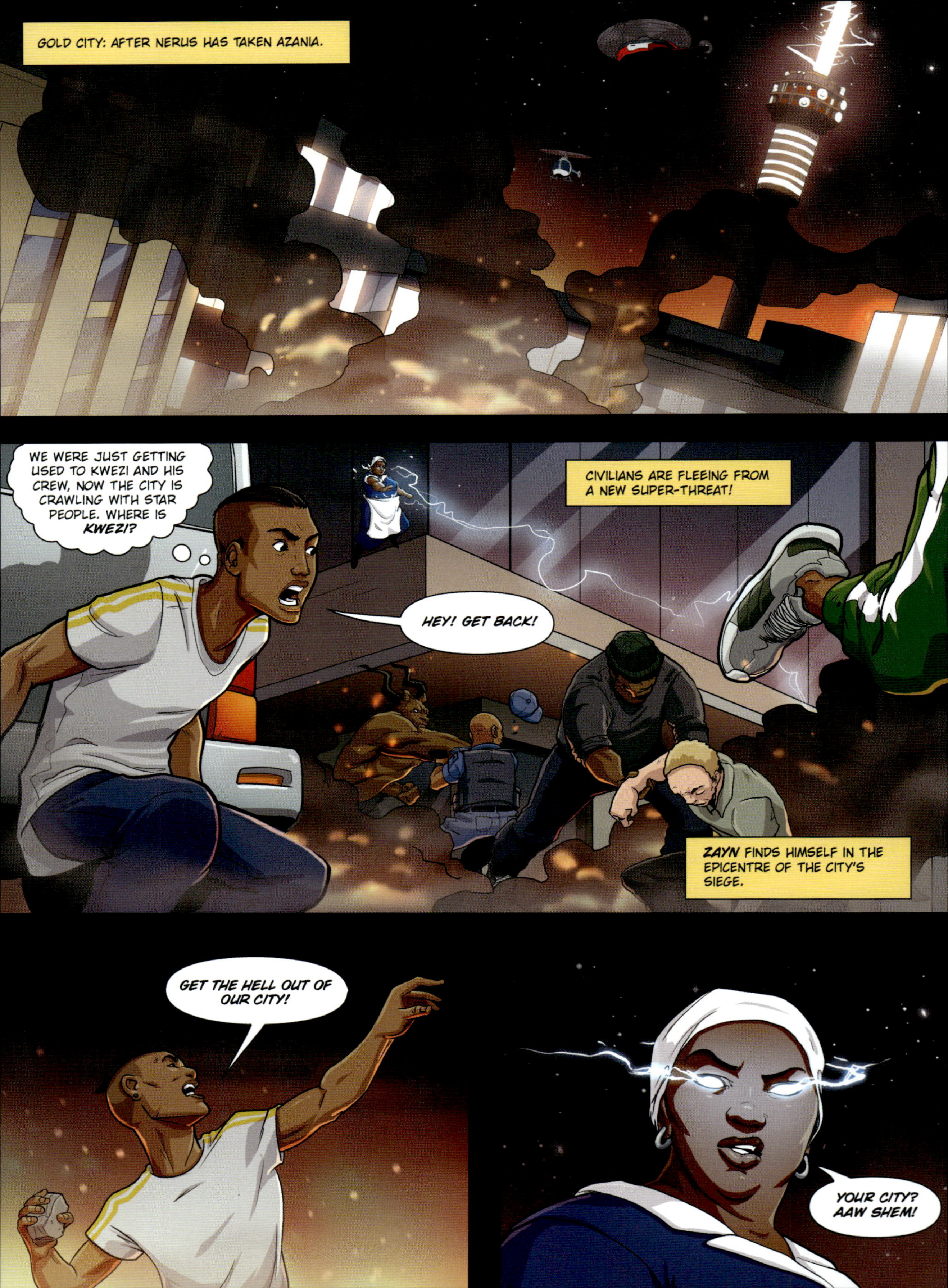
GOLD CITY: AFTER NERUS HAS TAKEN AZANIA.
WE WERE JUST GETTING USED TO KWEZI AND HIS CREW, NOW THE CITY IS CRAWLING WITH STAR PEOPLE. WHERE IS KWEZI?
CIVILIANS ARE FLEEING FROM A NEW SUPER-THREAT!
HEY! GET BACK!
ZAYN FINDS HIMSELF IN THE EPICENTRE OF THE CITY'S SIEGE.
GET THE HELL OUT OF OUR CITY!
YOUR CITY? AAW SHEM!

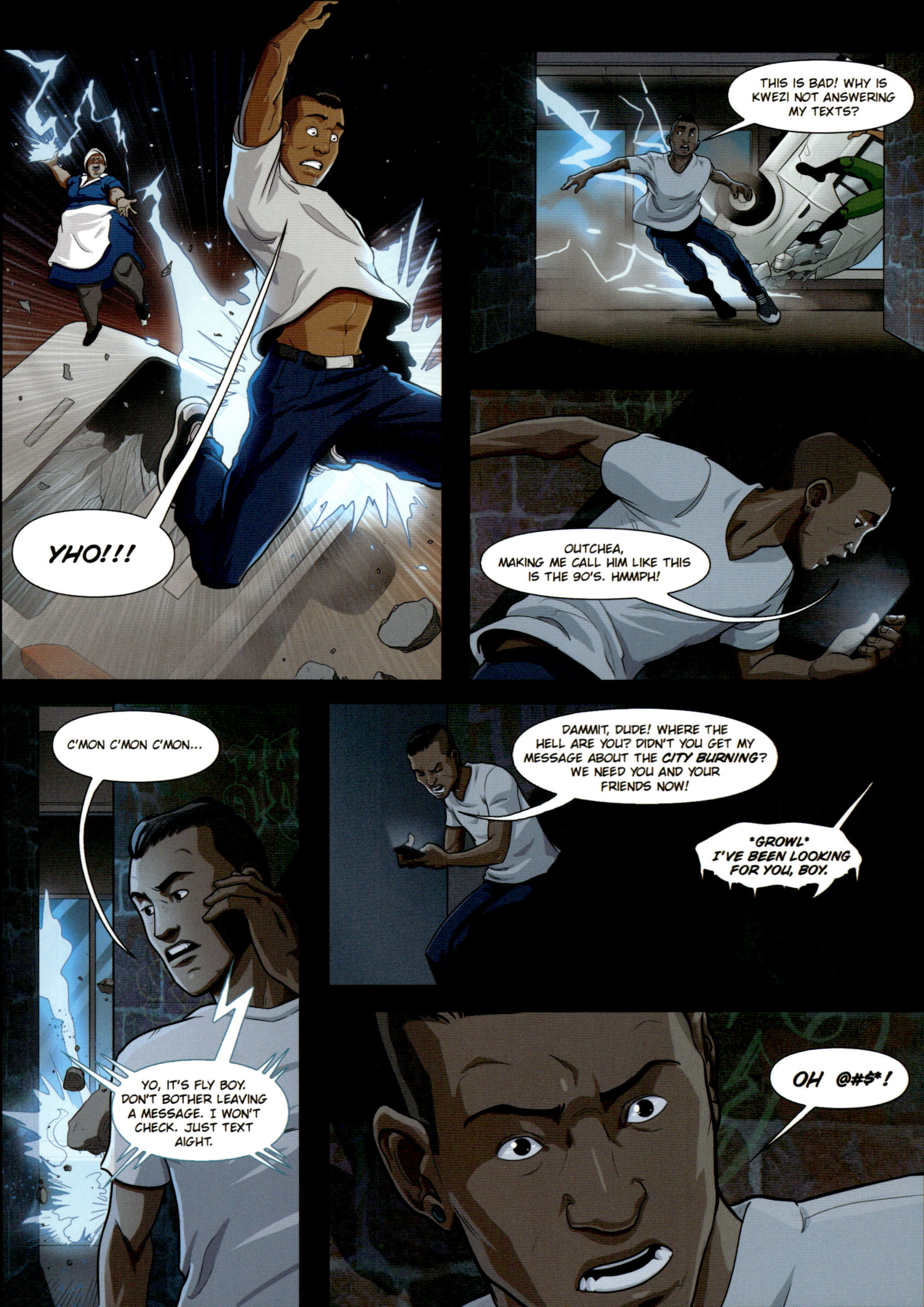
YHO!!!
THIS IS BAD! WHY IS KWEZI NOT ANSWERING MY TEXTS?
OUTCHEA, MAKING ME CALL HIM LIKE THIS IS THE 90'S. HMMPH!
C'MON C'MON C'MON...
YO, IT'S FLY BOY. DON'T BOTHER LEAVING A MESSAGE. I WON'T CHECK. JUST TEXT AIGHT.
DAMMIT, DUDE! WHERE THE HELL ARE YOU? DIDN'T YOU GET MY MESSAGE ABOUT THE CITY BURNING? WE NEED YOU AND YOUR FRIENDS NOW!
GROWL I'VE BEEN LOOKING FOR YOU, BOY.
OH @#$*!

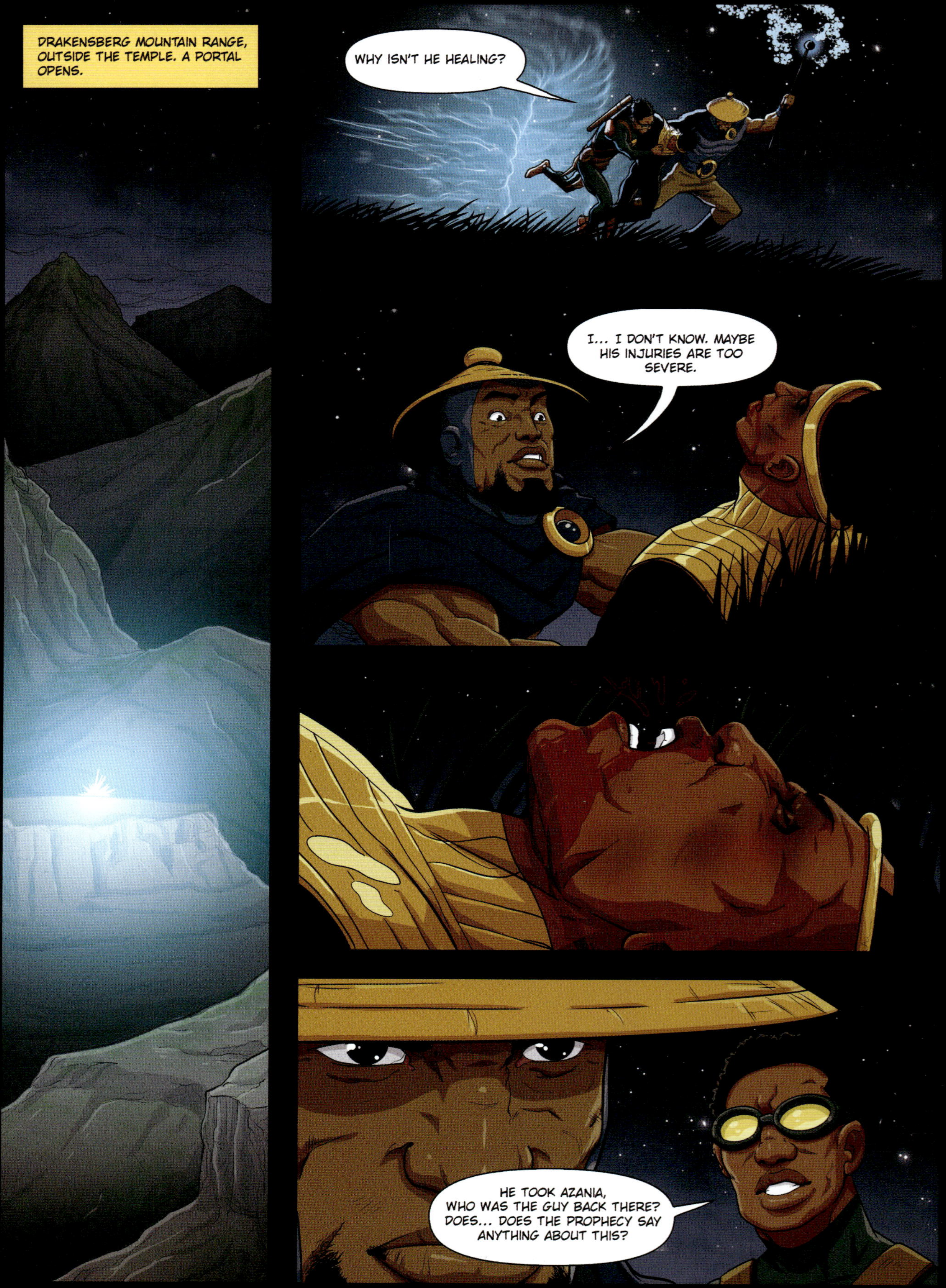
DRAKENSBERG MOUNTAIN RANGE, OUTSIDE THE TEMPLE. A PORTAL OPENS.
WHY ISN'T HE HEALING?
I... I DON'T KNOW. MAYBE HIS INJURIES ARE TOO SEVERE.
HE TOOK AZANIA, WHO WAS THE GUY BACK THERE? DOES... DOES THE PROPHECY SAY ANYTHING ABOUT THIS?

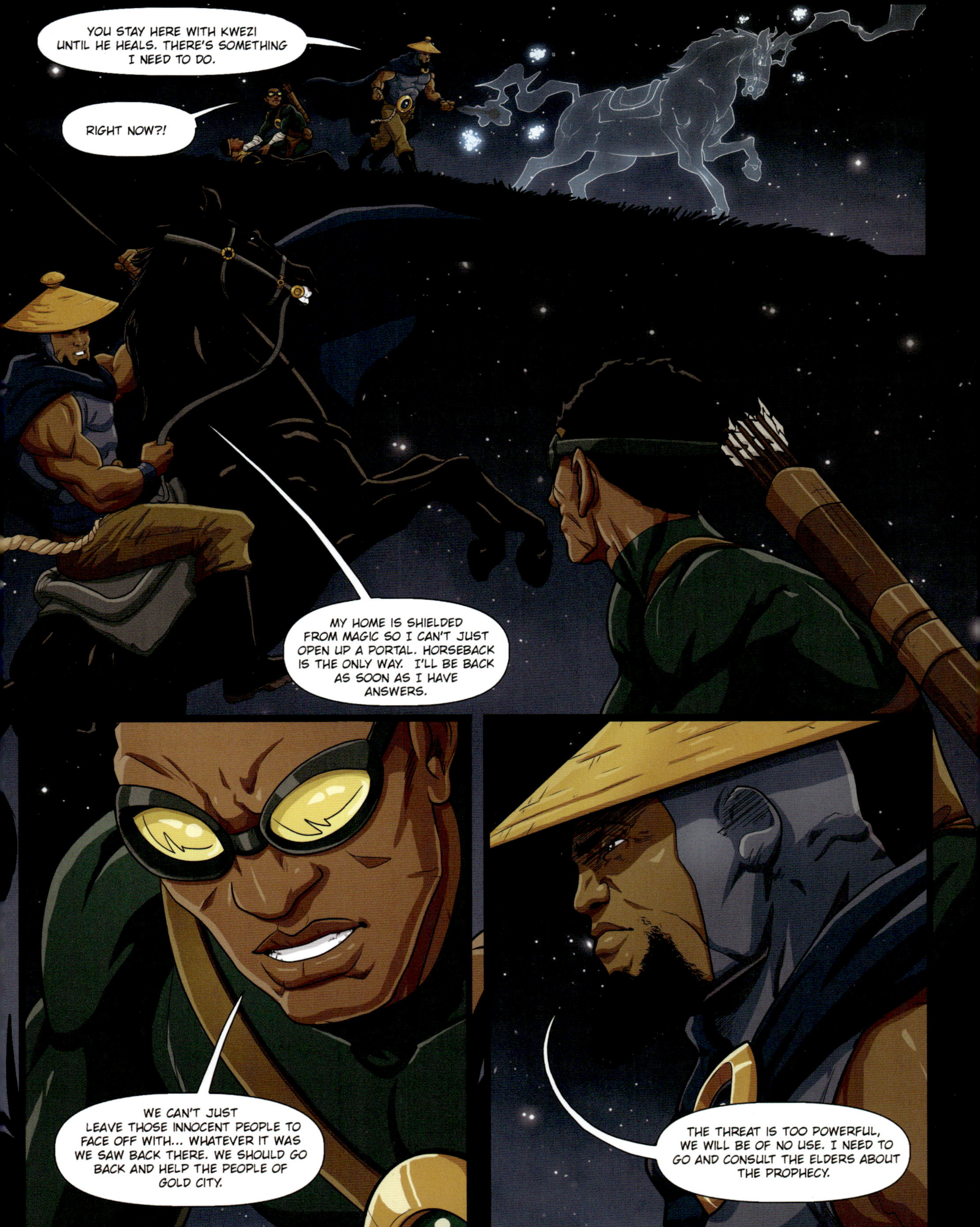
YOU STAY HERE WITH KWEZI UNTIL HE HEALS. THERE'S SOMETHING I NEED TO DO.
RIGHT NOW?!
MY HOME IS SHIELDED FROM MAGIC SO I CAN'T JUST OPEN UP A PORTAL. HORSEBACK IS THE ONLY WAY. I'LL BE BACK AS SOON AS I HAVE ANSWERS.
WE CAN'T JUST LEAVE THOSE INNOCENT PEOPLE TO FACE OFF WITH... WHATEVER IT WAS WE SAW BACK THERE. WE SHOULD GO BACK AND HELP THE PEOPLE OF GOLD CITY.
THE THREAT IS TOO POWERFUL, WE WILL BE OF NO USE. I NEED TO GO AND CONSULT THE ELDERS ABOUT THE PROPHECY.

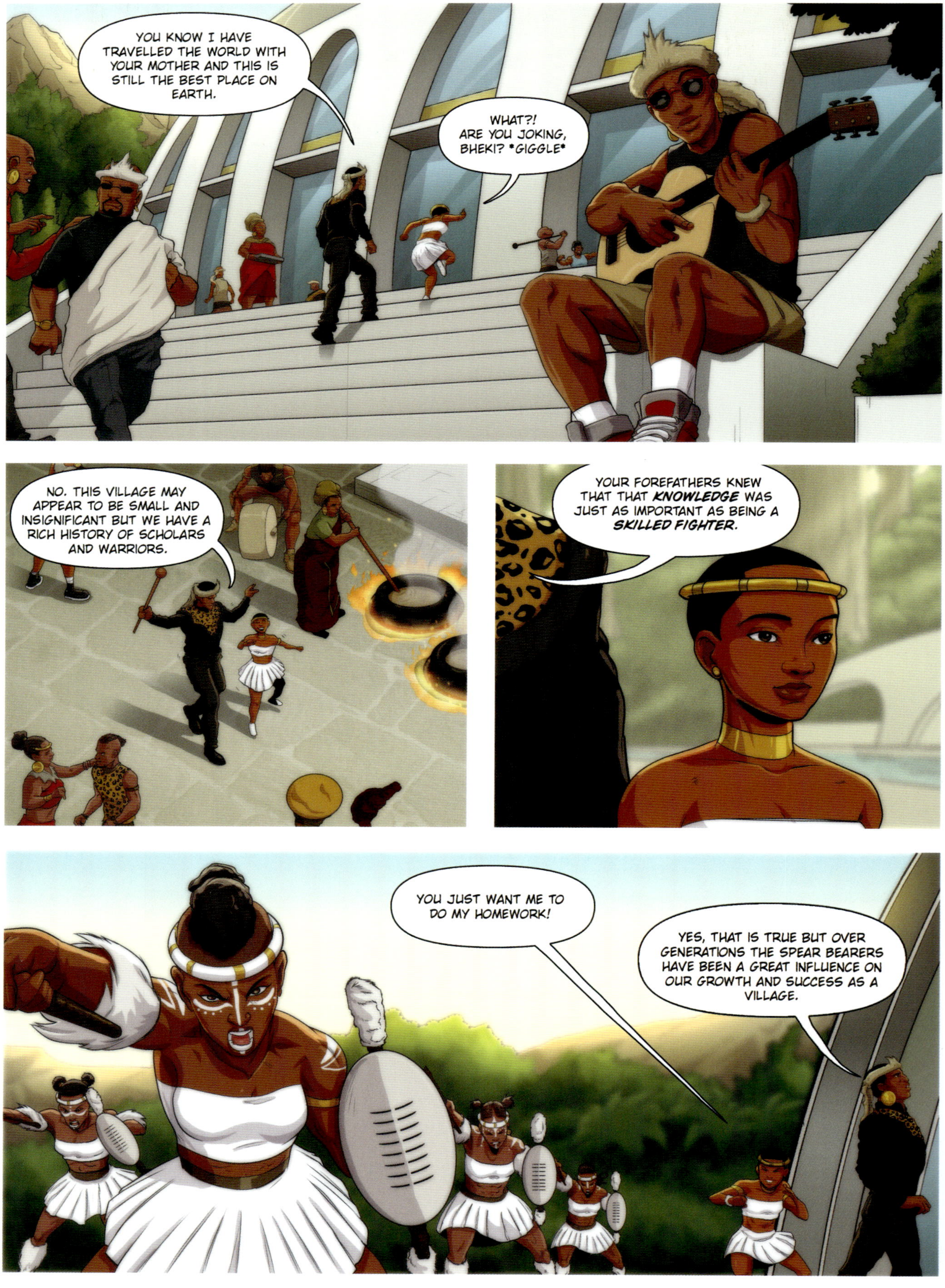
YOU KNOW I HAVE TRAVELLED THE WORLD WITH YOUR MOTHER AND THIS IS STILL THE BEST PLACE ON EARTH.
WHAT?! ARE YOU JOKING, BHEKI? *GIGGLE*
NO. THIS VILLAGE MAY APPEAR TO BE SMALL AND INSIGNIFICANT BUT WE HAVE A RICH HISTORY OF SCHOLARS AND WARRIORS.
YOUR FOREFATHERS KNEW THAT THAT KNOWLEDGE WAS JUST AS IMPORTANT AS BEING A SKILLED FIGHTER.
YOU JUST WANT ME TO DO MY HOMEWORK!
YES, THAT IS TRUE BUT OVER GENERATIONS THE SPEAR BEARERS HAVE BEEN A GREAT INFLUENCE ON OUR GROWTH AND SUCCESS AS A VILLAGE.

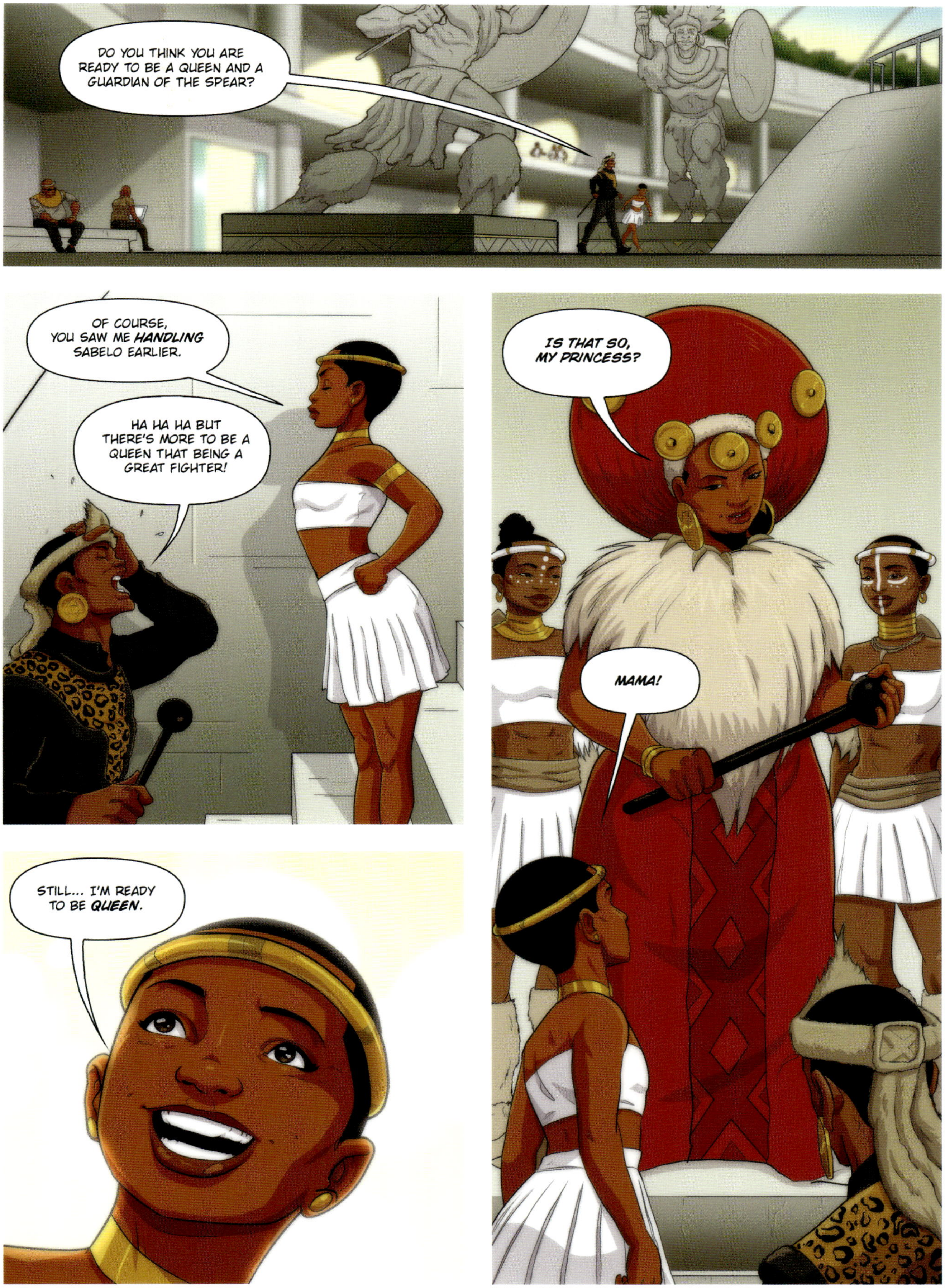
DO YOU THINK YOU ARE READY TO BE A QUEEN AND A GUARDIAN OF THE SPEAR?
OF COURSE, YOU SAW ME HANDLING SABELO EARLIER.
HA HA HA BUT THERE'S MORE TO BE A QUEEN THAT BEING A GREAT FIGHTER!
STILL... I'M READY TO BE QUEEN.
IS THAT SO, MY PRINCESS?
MAMA!

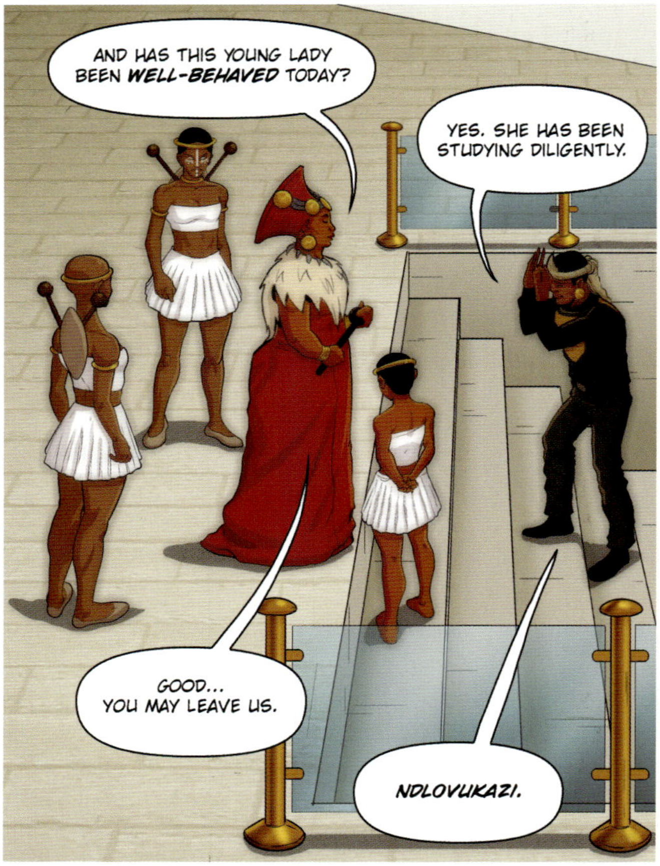
AND HAS THIS YOUNG LADY BEEN ***WELL-BEHAVED*** TODAY?
YES. SHE HAS BEEN STUDYING DILIGENTLY.
GOOD... YOU MAY LEAVE US.
NDLOVUKAZI.

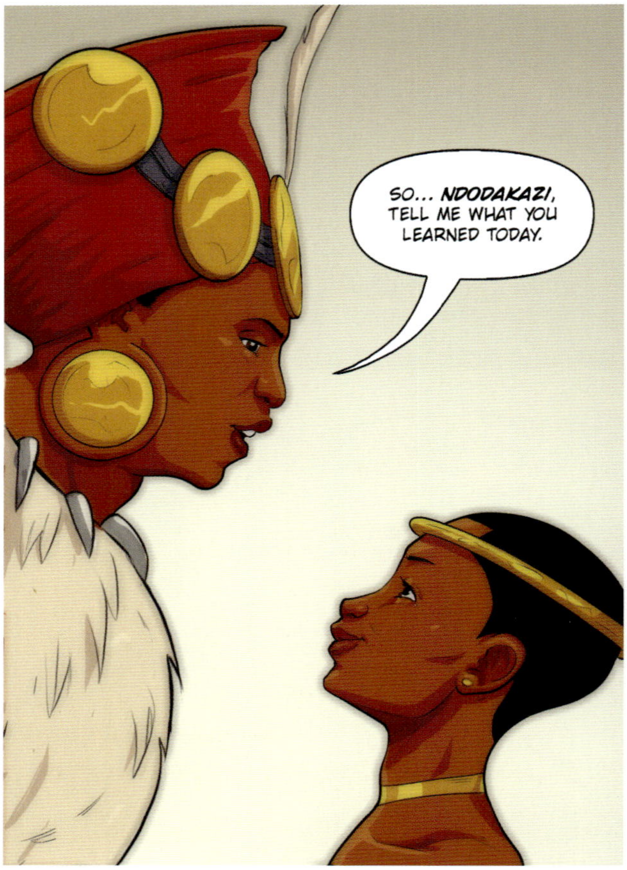
SO... ***NDODAKAZI***, TELL ME WHAT YOU LEARNED TODAY.

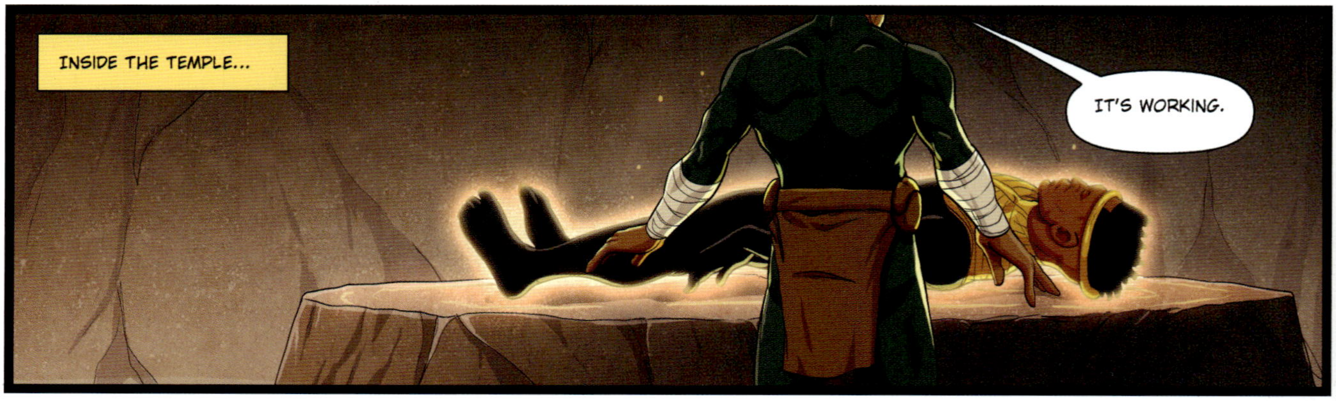
INSIDE THE TEMPLE...
IT'S WORKING.

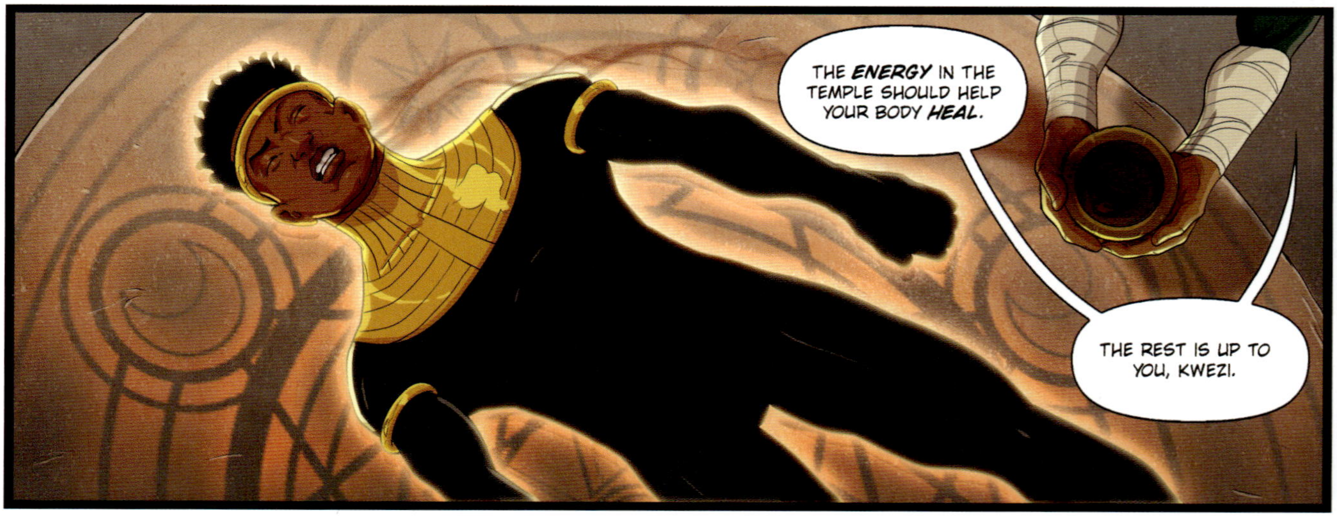
THE ***ENERGY*** IN THE TEMPLE SHOULD HELP YOUR BODY ***HEAL***.
THE REST IS UP TO YOU, KWEZI.

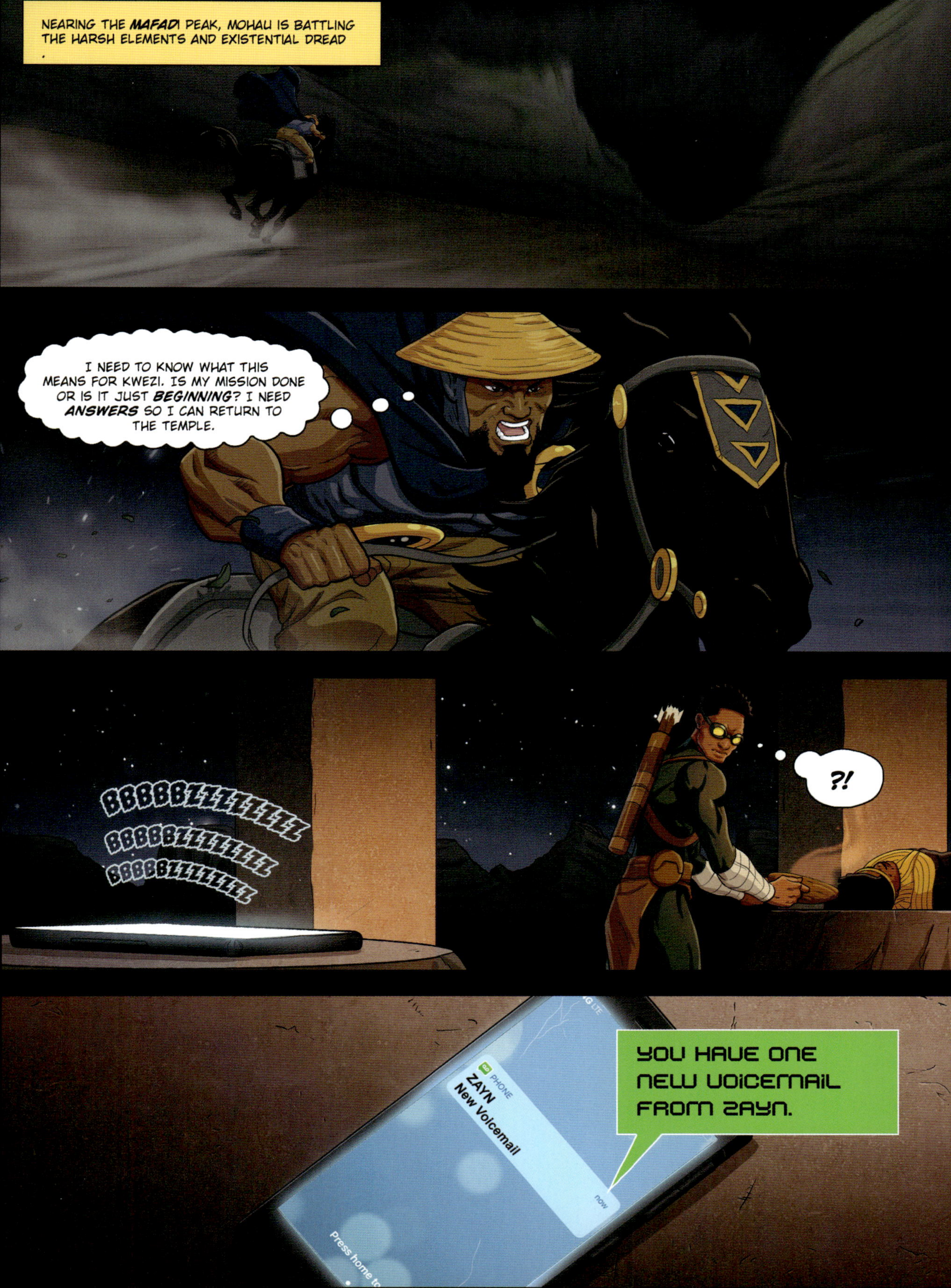
NEARING THE MAFADI PEAK, MOHAU IS BATTLING THE HARSH ELEMENTS AND EXISTENTIAL DREAD
I NEED TO KNOW WHAT THIS MEANS FOR KWEZI. IS MY MISSION DONE OR IS IT JUST BEGINNING? I NEED ANSWERS SO I CAN RETURN TO THE TEMPLE.
BBBBBBZZZZZZZZZ
BBBBBZZZZZZZZZ
BBBBBZZZZZZZZ
?!
PHONE
ZAYN
New Voicemail
now
YOU HAVE ONE NEW VOICEMAIL FROM ZAYN.

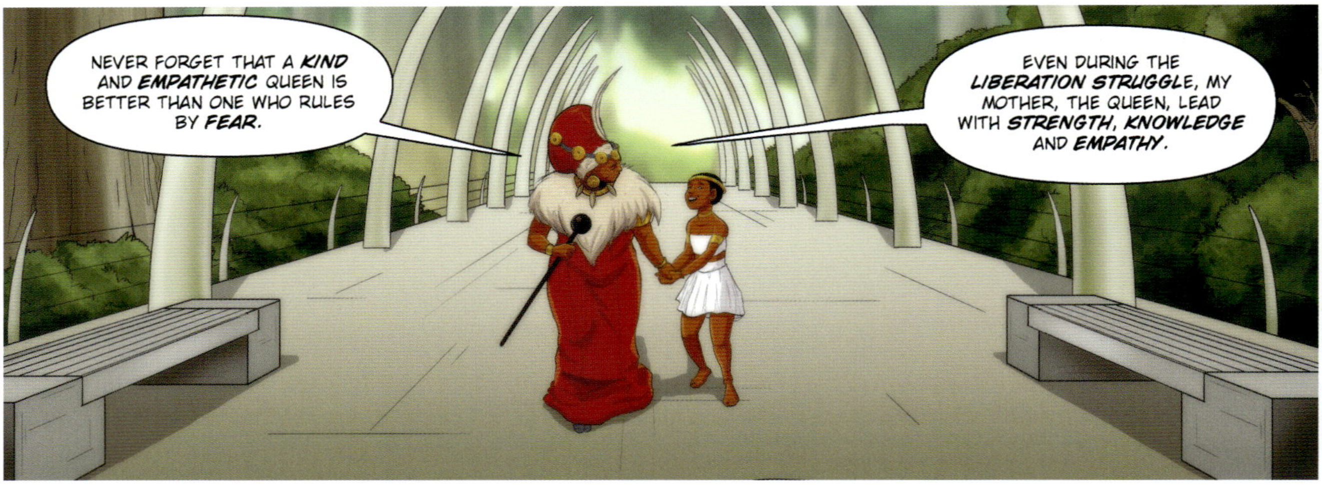
NEVER FORGET THAT A KIND AND EMPATHETIC QUEEN IS BETTER THAN ONE WHO RULES BY FEAR.
EVEN DURING THE LIBERATION STRUGGLE, MY MOTHER, THE QUEEN, LEAD WITH STRENGTH, KNOWLEDGE AND EMPATHY.

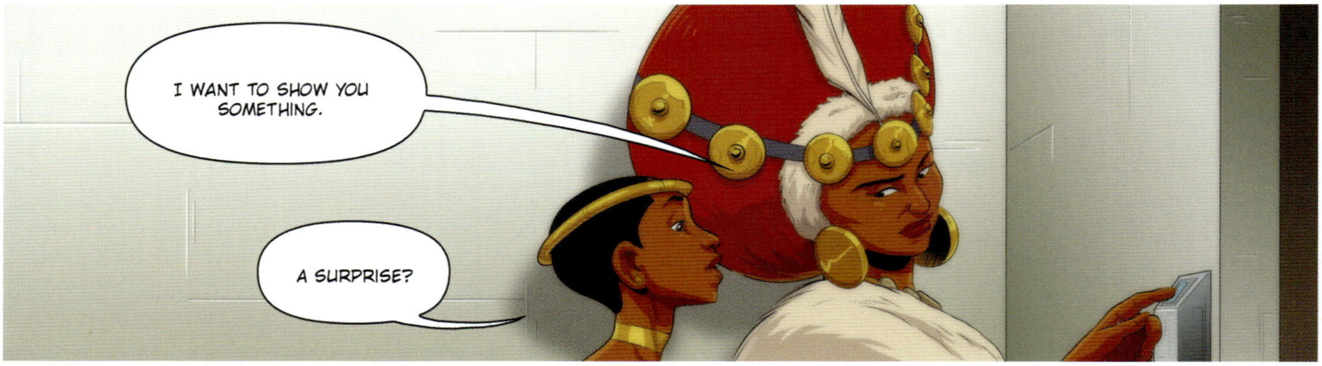
I WANT TO SHOW YOU SOMETHING.
A SURPRISE?

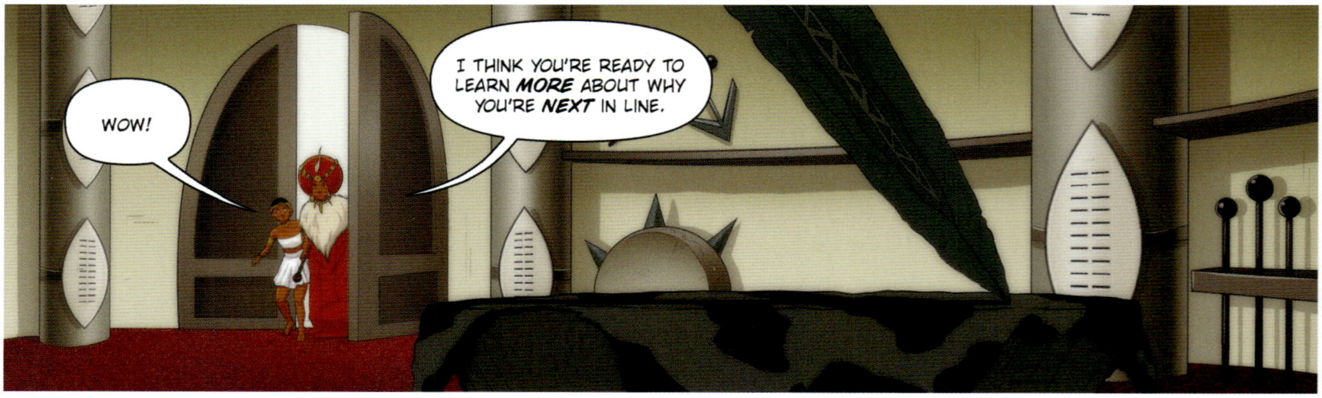
WOW!
I THINK YOU'RE READY TO LEARN MORE ABOUT WHY YOU'RE NEXT IN LINE.

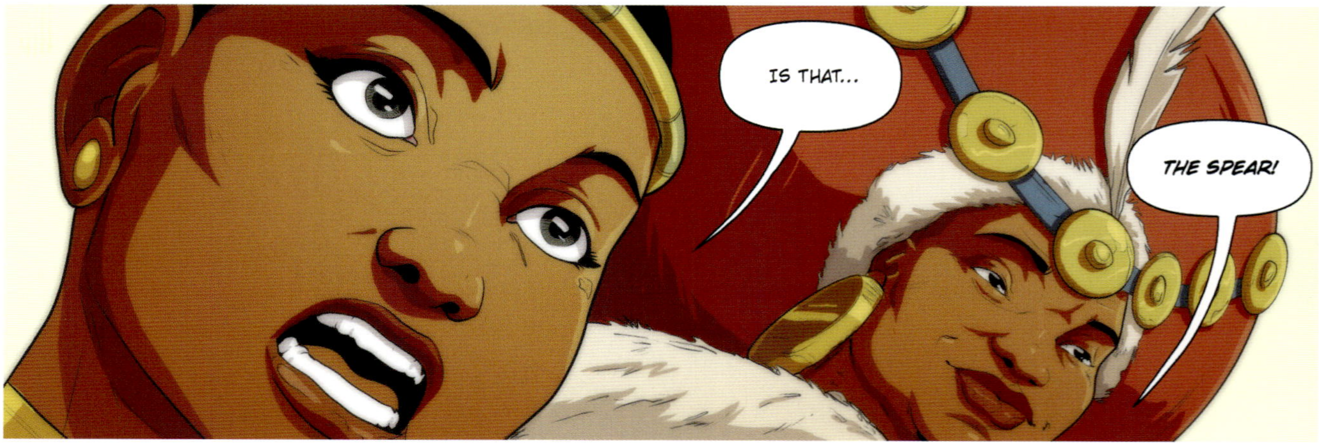
IS THAT...
THE SPEAR!

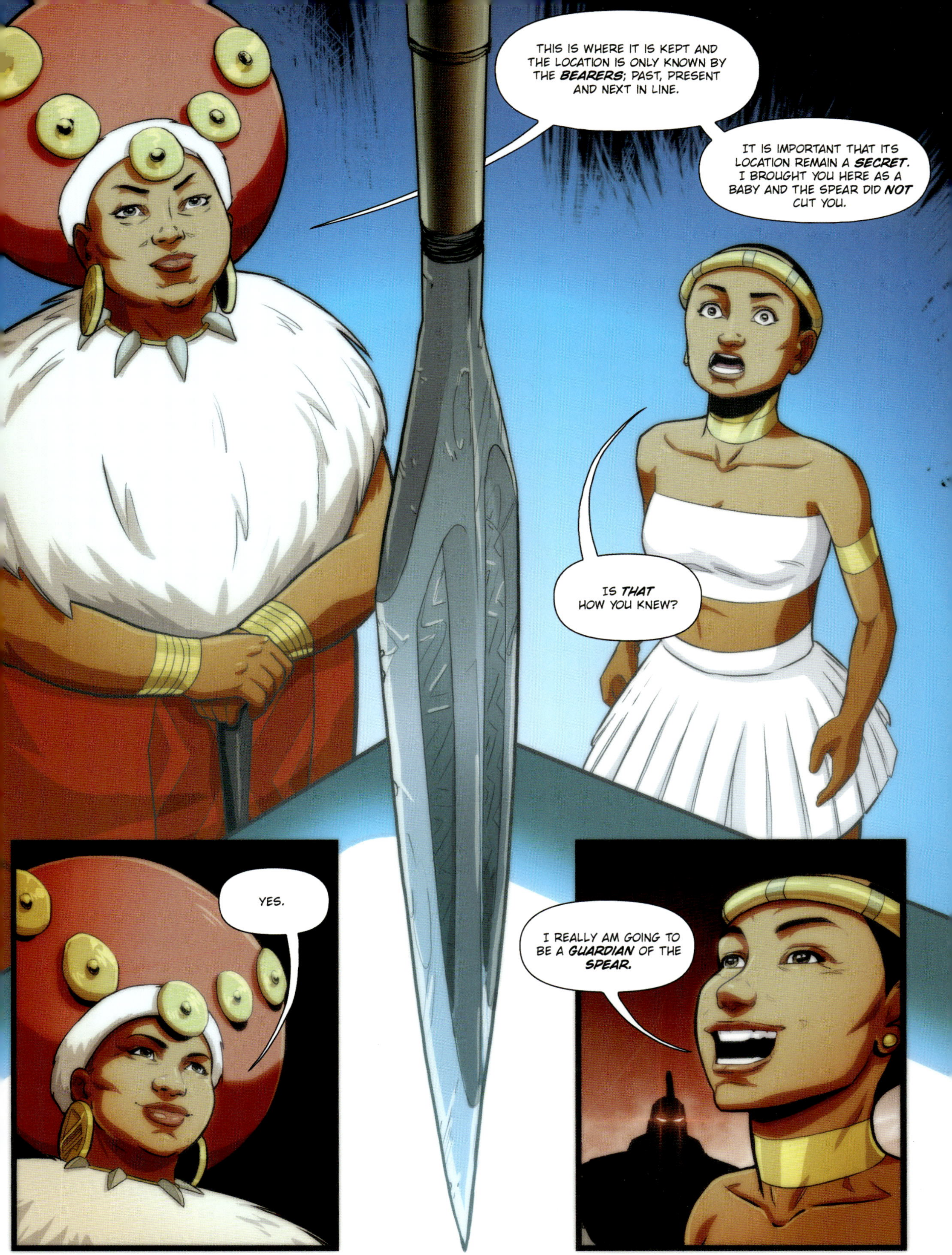
THIS IS WHERE IT IS KEPT AND THE LOCATION IS ONLY KNOWN BY THE BEARERS; PAST, PRESENT AND NEXT IN LINE.
IT IS IMPORTANT THAT ITS LOCATION REMAIN A SECRET. I BROUGHT YOU HERE AS A BABY AND THE SPEAR DID NOT CUT YOU.
IS THAT HOW YOU KNEW?
YES.
I REALLY AM GOING TO BE A GUARDIAN OF THE SPEAR.

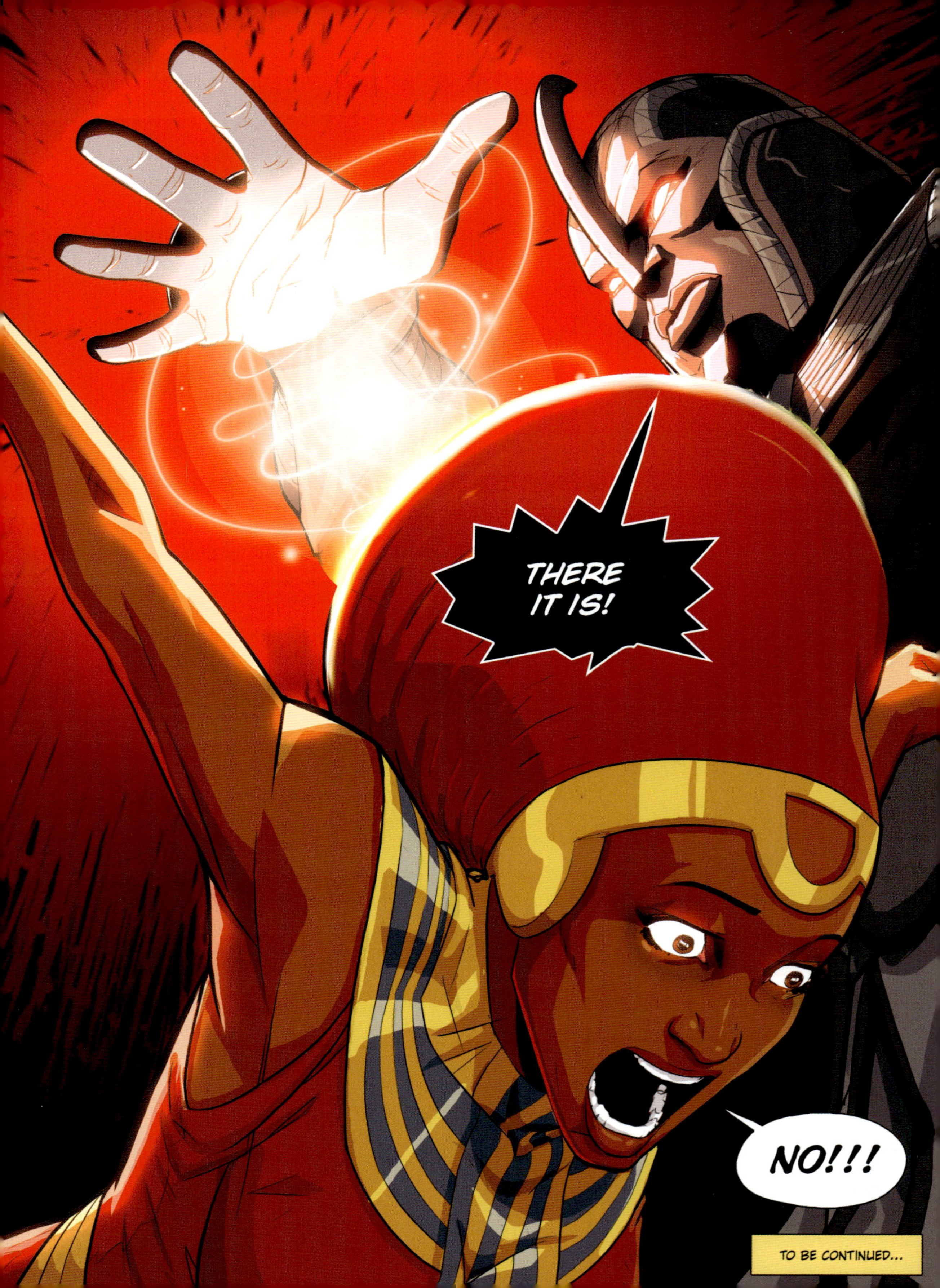
THERE IT IS!
NO!!!
TO BE CONTINUED...

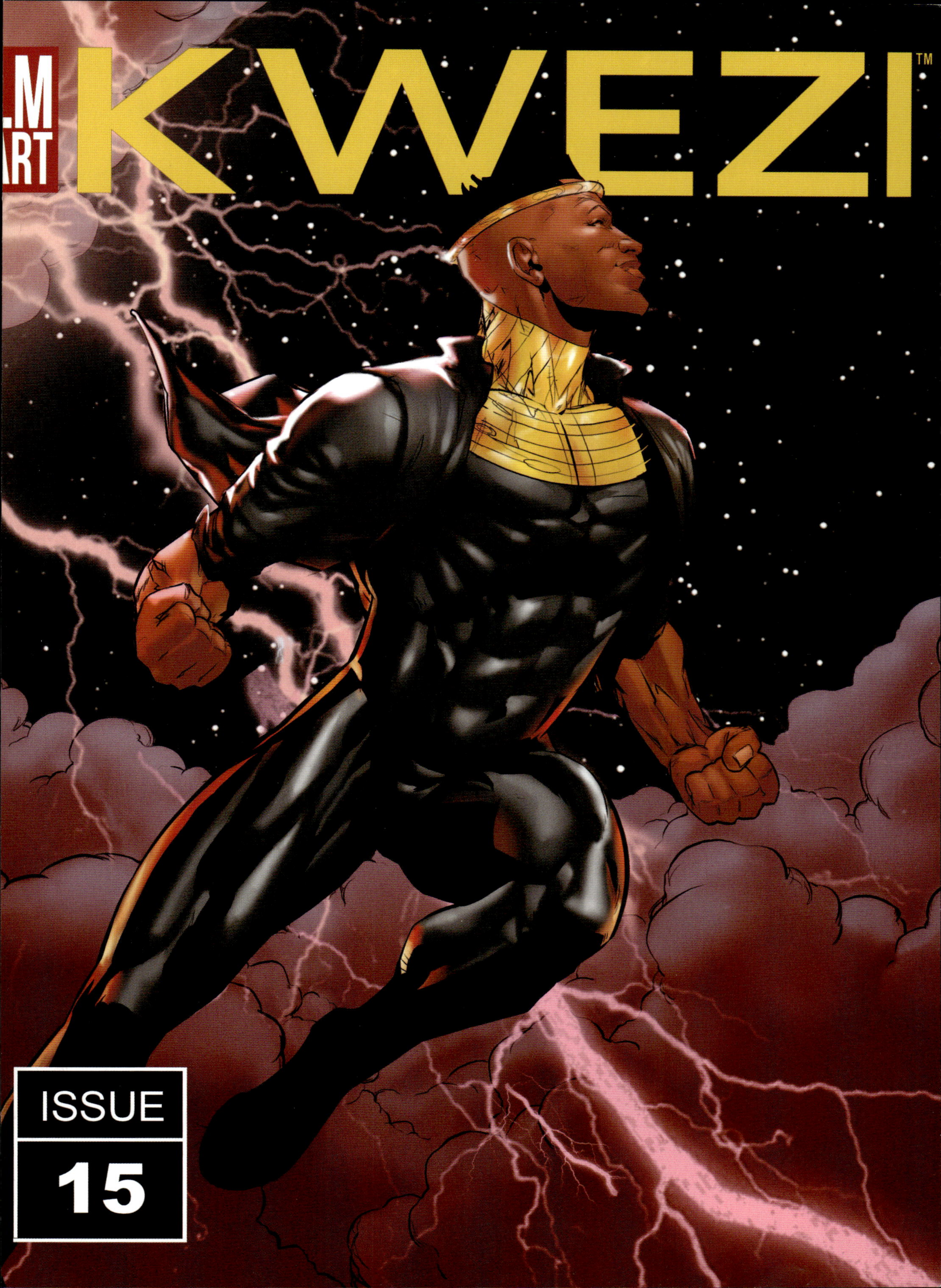
KWEZI™
ISSUE
15

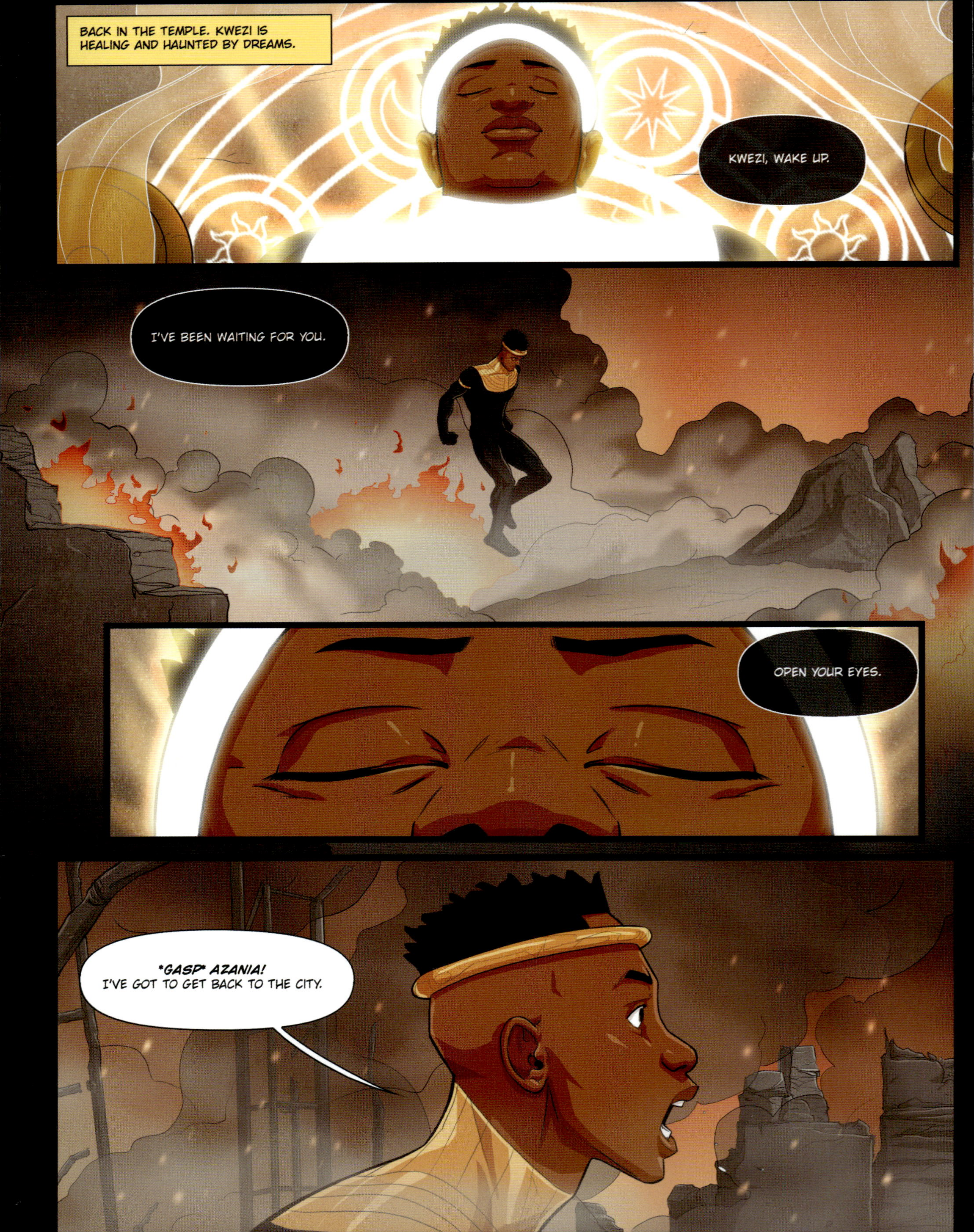
BACK IN THE TEMPLE. KWEZI IS HEALING AND HAUNTED BY DREAMS.
KWEZI, WAKE UP.
I'VE BEEN WAITING FOR YOU.
OPEN YOUR EYES.
GASP AZANIA!
I'VE GOT TO GET BACK TO THE CITY.

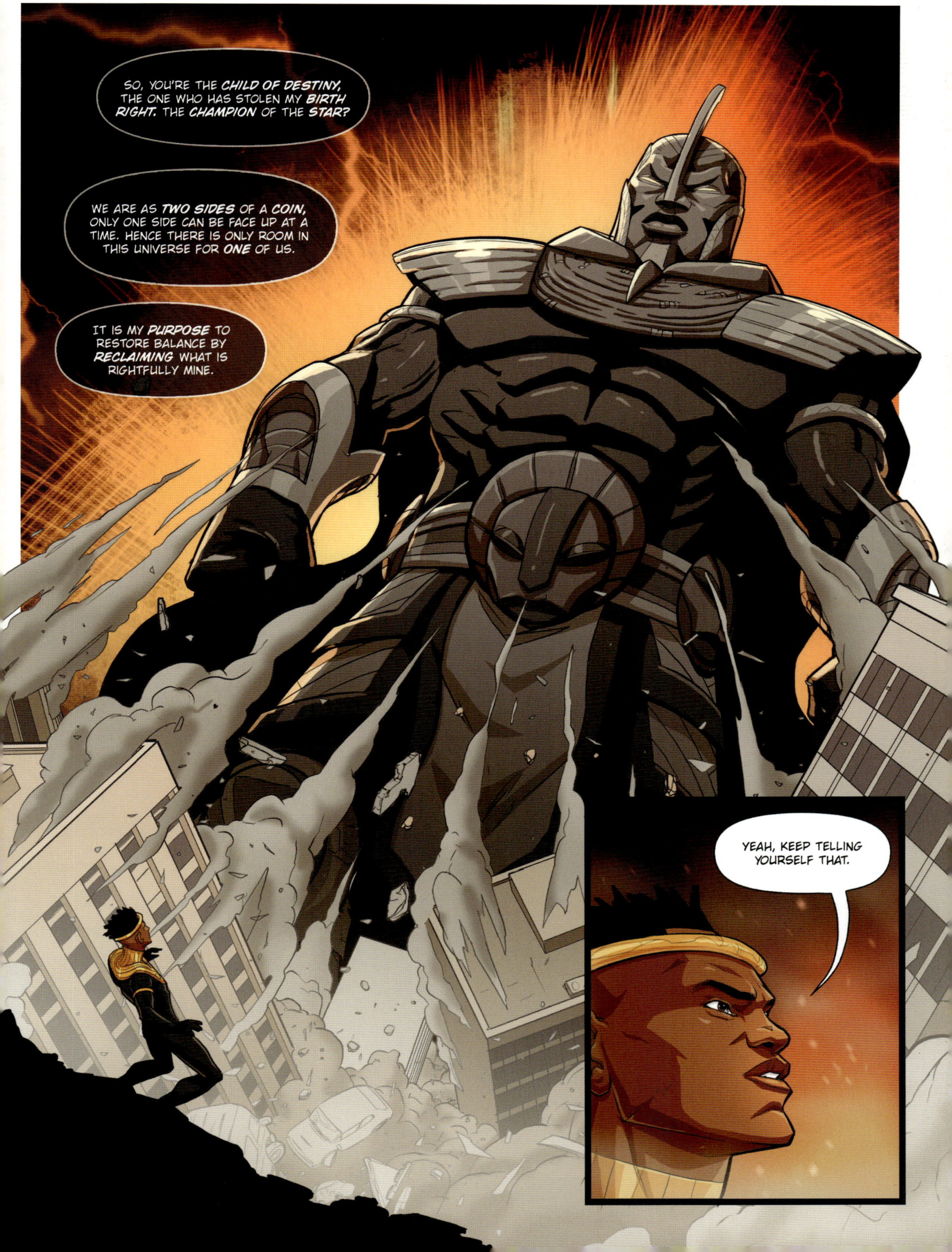
SO, YOU'RE THE CHILD OF DESTINY, THE ONE WHO HAS STOLEN MY BIRTH RIGHT. THE CHAMPION OF THE STAR?
WE ARE AS TWO SIDES OF A COIN, ONLY ONE SIDE CAN BE FACE UP AT A TIME. HENCE THERE IS ONLY ROOM IN THIS UNIVERSE FOR ONE OF US.
IT IS MY PURPOSE TO RESTORE BALANCE BY RECLAIMING WHAT IS RIGHTFULLY MINE.
YEAH, KEEP TELLING YOURSELF THAT.

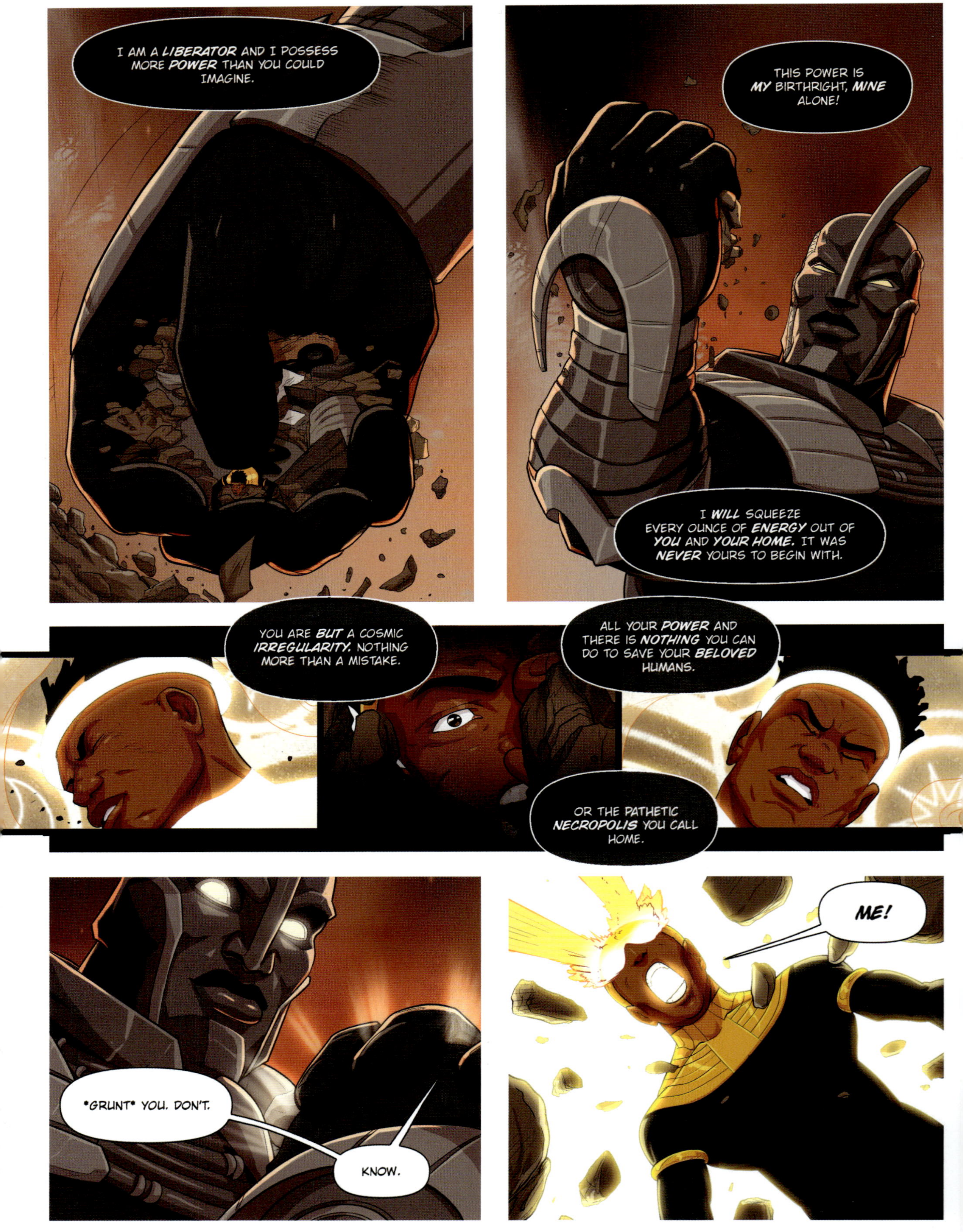
I AM A LIBERATOR AND I POSSESS MORE POWER THAN YOU COULD IMAGINE.
THIS POWER IS MY BIRTHRIGHT, MINE ALONE!
I WILL SQUEEZE EVERY OUNCE OF ENERGY OUT OF YOU AND YOUR HOME. IT WAS NEVER YOURS TO BEGIN WITH.
YOU ARE BUT A COSMIC IRREGULARITY. NOTHING MORE THAN A MISTAKE.
ALL YOUR POWER AND THERE IS NOTHING YOU CAN DO TO SAVE YOUR BELOVED HUMANS.
OR THE PATHETIC NECROPOLIS YOU CALL HOME.
GRUNT YOU. DON'T.
KNOW.
ME!

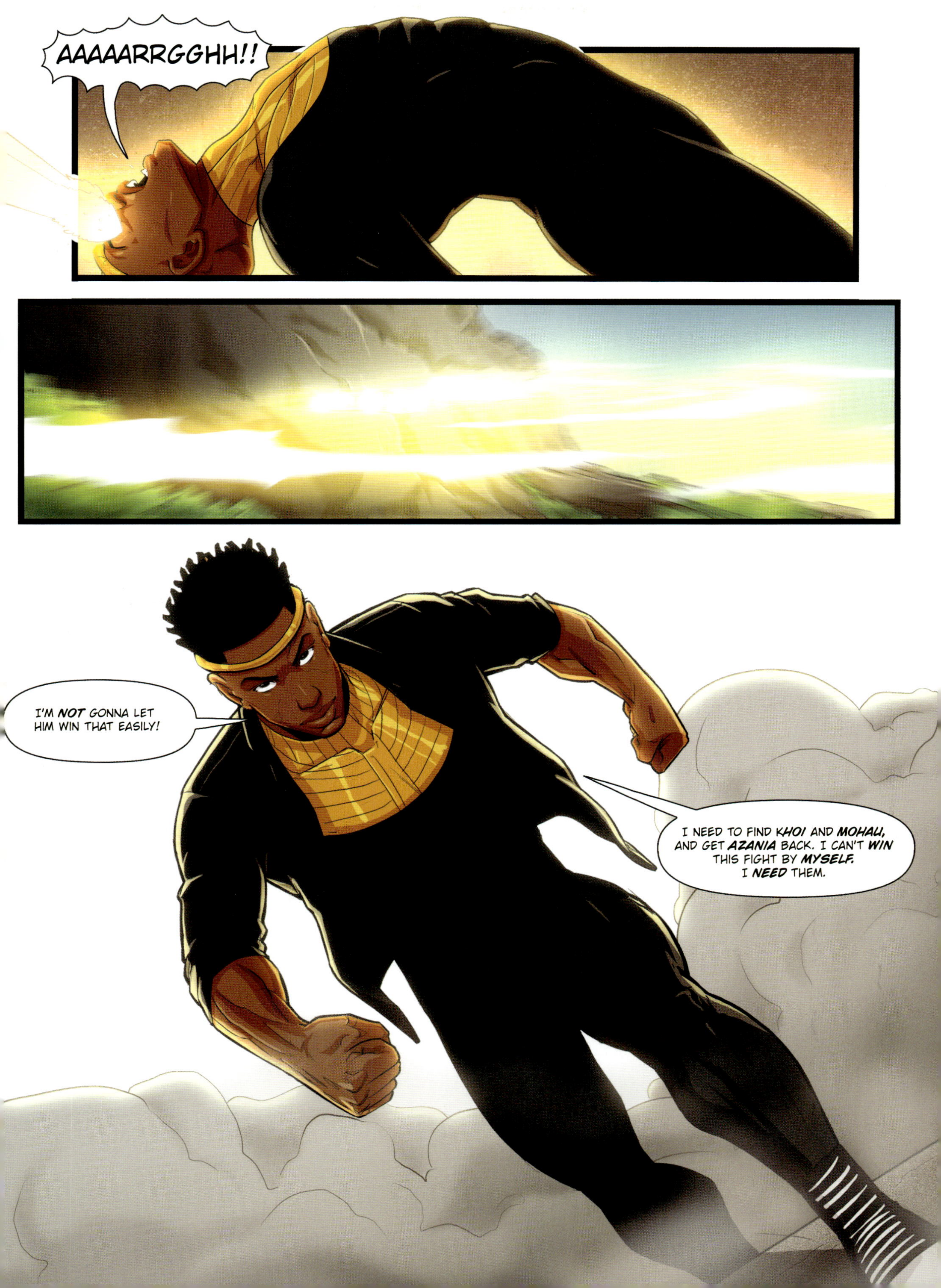
AAAAARRGGHH!!
I'M NOT GONNA LET HIM WIN THAT EASILY!
I NEED TO FIND KHOI AND MOHAU, AND GET AZANIA BACK. I CAN'T WIN THIS FIGHT BY MYSELF. I NEED THEM.

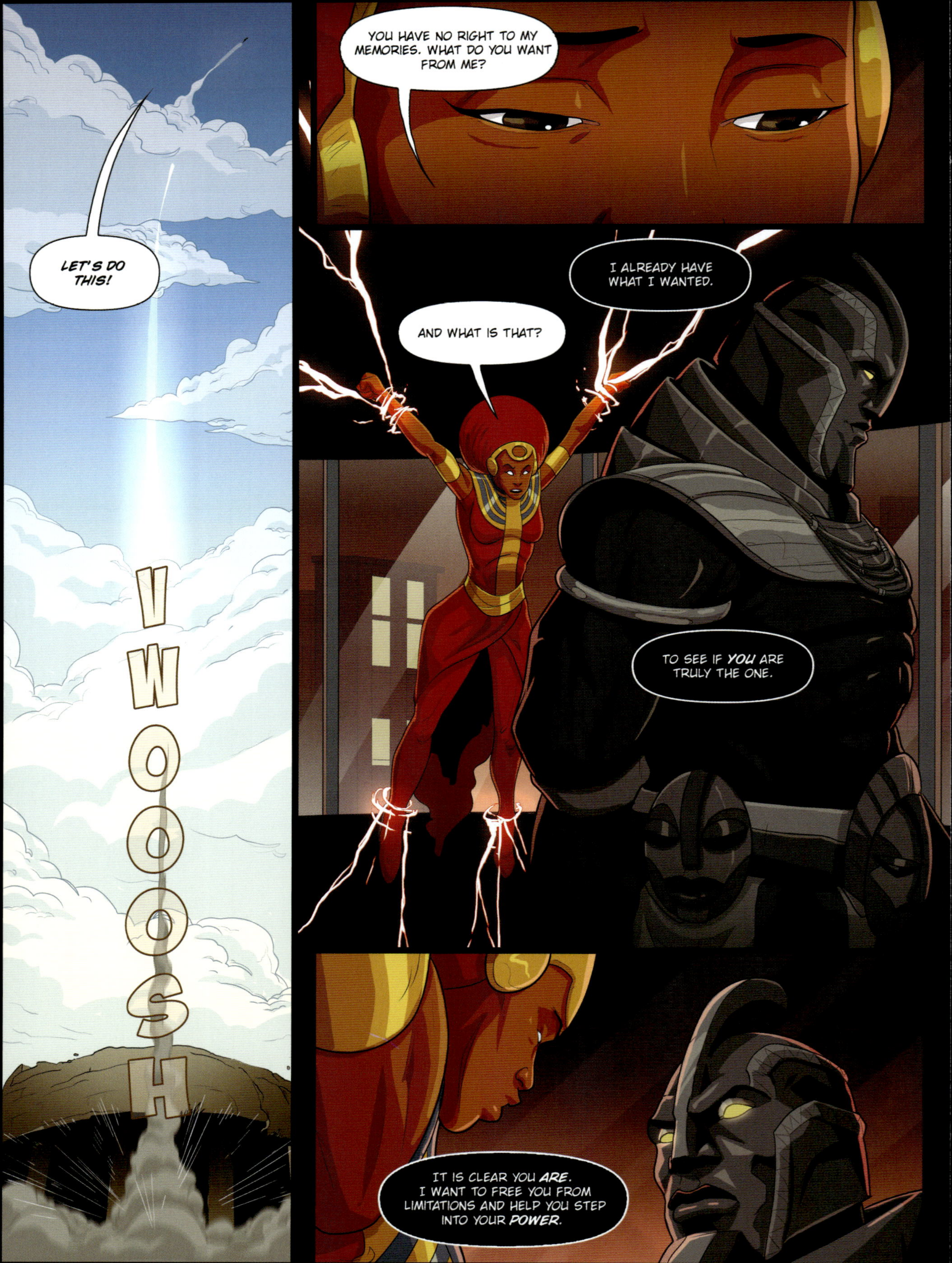
LET'S DO THIS!
VWOOOSH
YOU HAVE NO RIGHT TO MY MEMORIES. WHAT DO YOU WANT FROM ME?
I ALREADY HAVE WHAT I WANTED.
AND WHAT IS THAT?
TO SEE IF *YOU* ARE TRULY THE ONE.
IT IS CLEAR YOU *ARE*. I WANT TO FREE YOU FROM LIMITATIONS AND HELP YOU STEP INTO YOUR *POWER*.

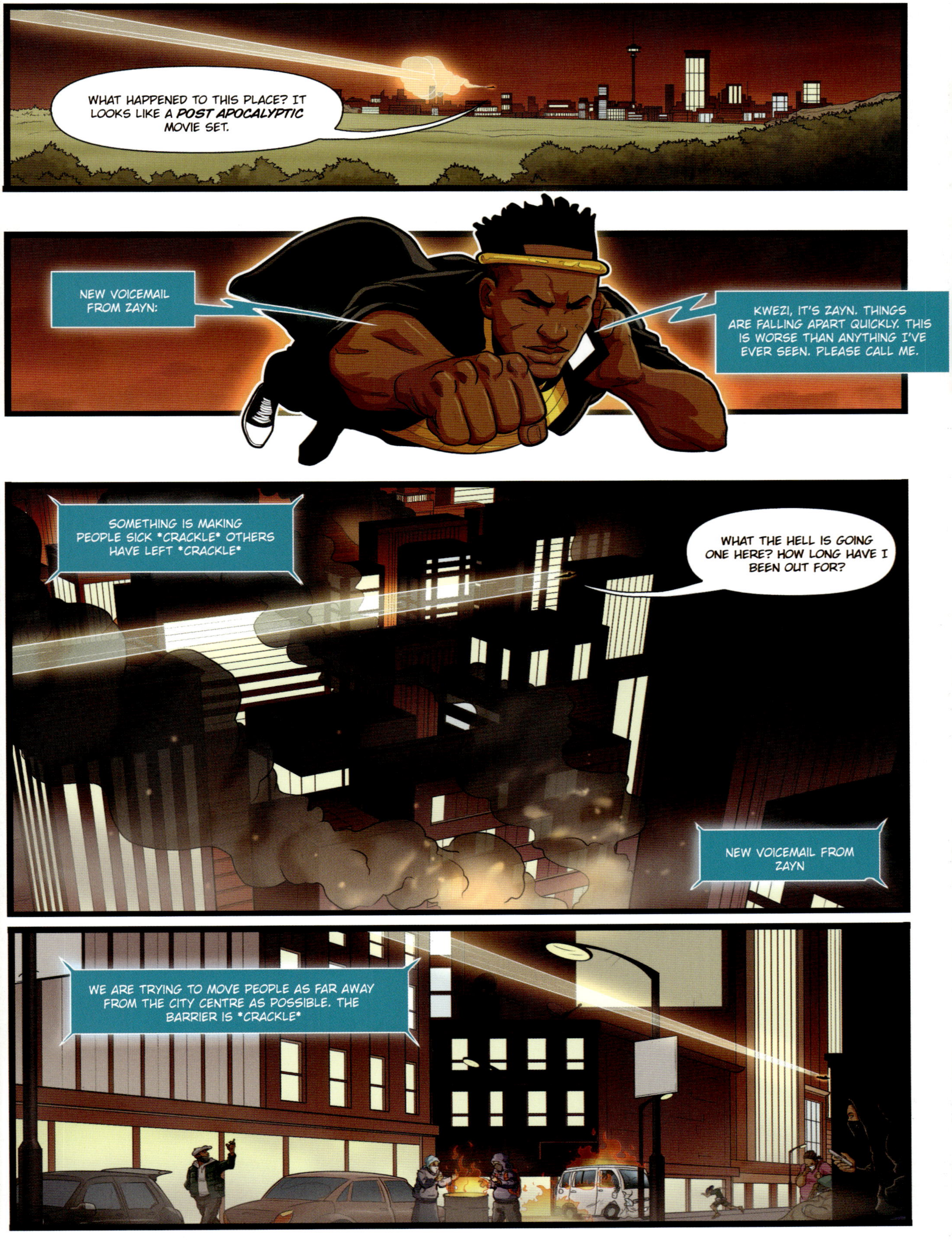
WHAT HAPPENED TO THIS PLACE? IT LOOKS LIKE A POST APOCALYPTIC MOVIE SET.
NEW VOICEMAIL FROM ZAYN:
KWEZI, IT'S ZAYN. THINGS ARE FALLING APART QUICKLY. THIS IS WORSE THAN ANYTHING I'VE EVER SEEN. PLEASE CALL ME.
SOMETHING IS MAKING PEOPLE SICK *CRACKLE* OTHERS HAVE LEFT *CRACKLE*
WHAT THE HELL IS GOING ONE HERE? HOW LONG HAVE I BEEN OUT FOR?
NEW VOICEMAIL FROM ZAYN
WE ARE TRYING TO MOVE PEOPLE AS FAR AWAY FROM THE CITY CENTRE AS POSSIBLE. THE BARRIER IS *CRACKLE*

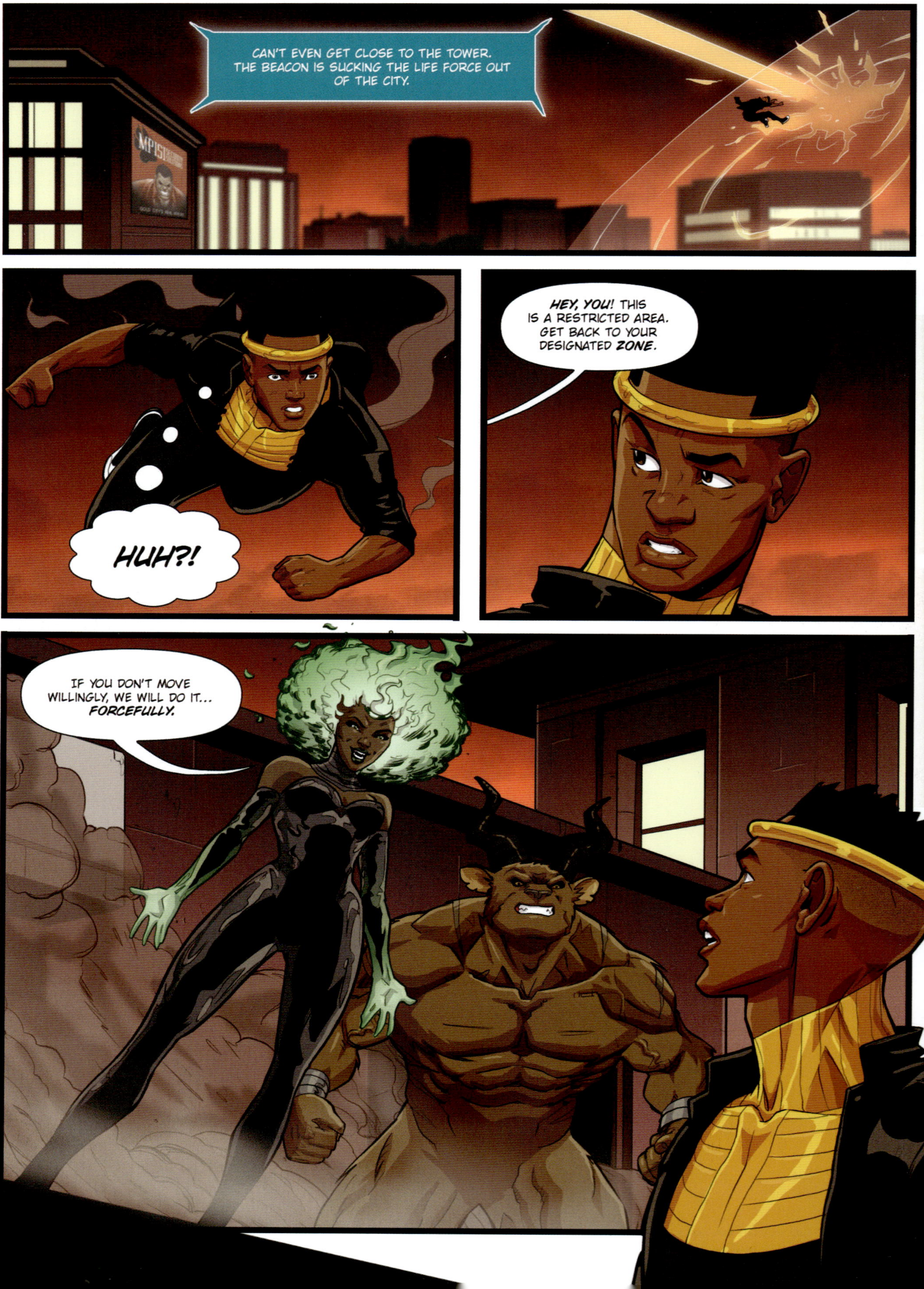
CAN'T EVEN GET CLOSE TO THE TOWER. THE BEACON IS SUCKING THE LIFE FORCE OUT OF THE CITY.
HUH?!
HEY, YOU! THIS IS A RESTRICTED AREA. GET BACK TO YOUR DESIGNATED ZONE.
IF YOU DON'T MOVE WILLINGLY, WE WILL DO IT... FORCEFULLY.

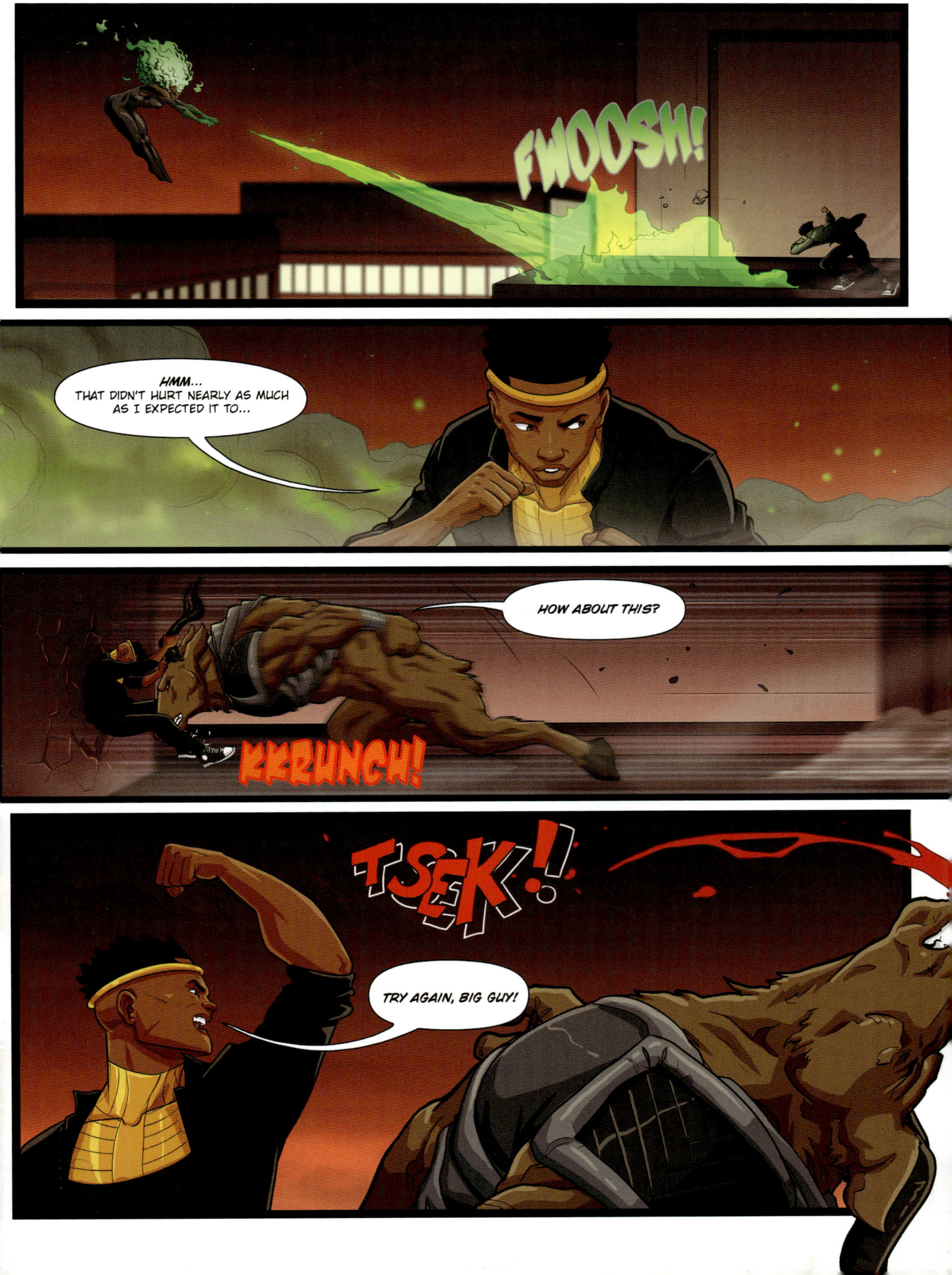
FWOOSH!
HMM... THAT DIDN'T HURT NEARLY AS MUCH AS I EXPECTED IT TO...
HOW ABOUT THIS?
KKRUNCH!
TSEK!!
TRY AGAIN, BIG GUY!

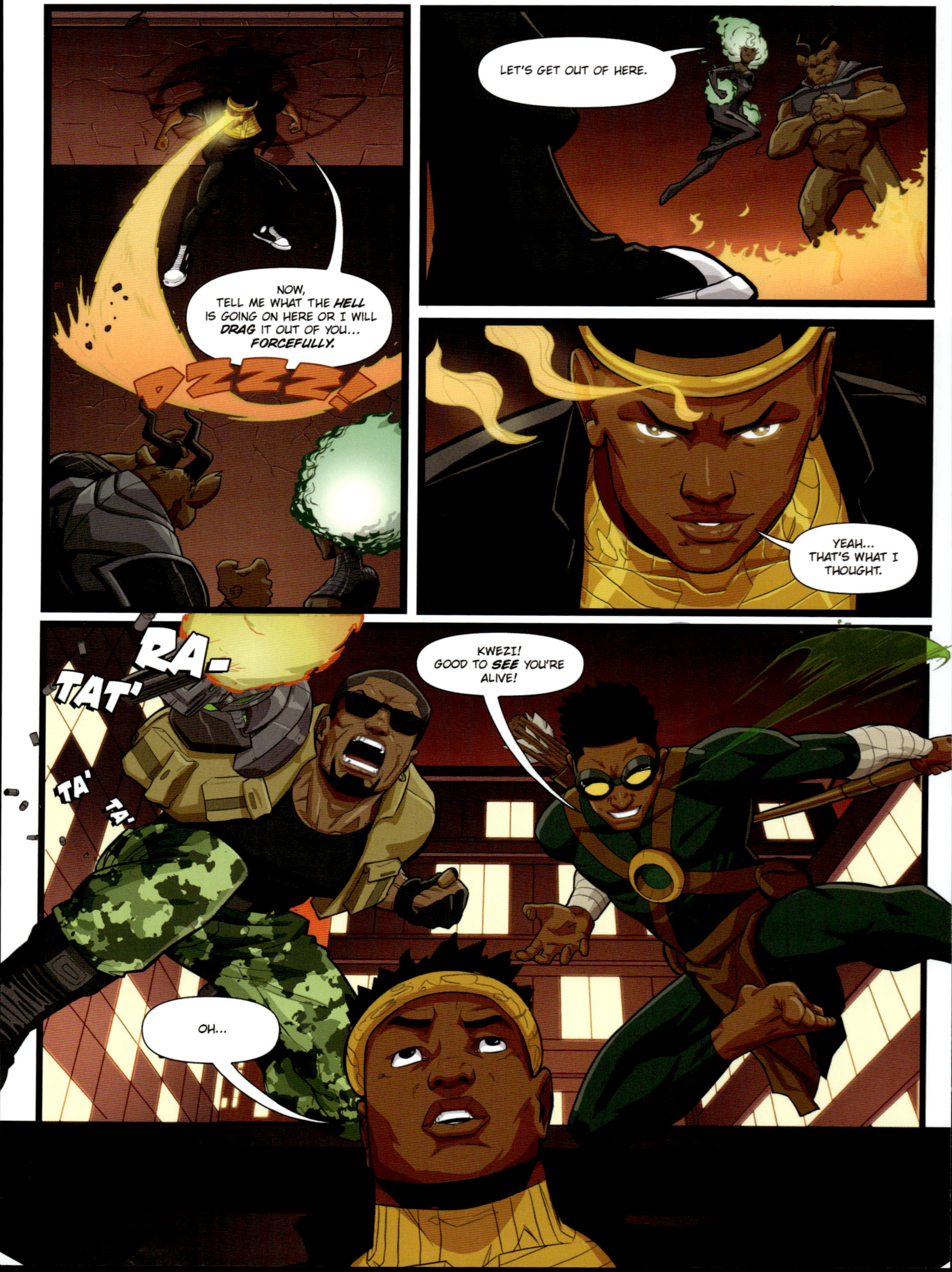
NOW, TELL ME WHAT THE HELL IS GOING ON HERE OR I WILL DRAG IT OUT OF YOU... FORCEFULLY.
DZZZ!
LET'S GET OUT OF HERE.
YEAH... THAT'S WHAT I THOUGHT.
RA-TAT'
TA' TA'
KWEZI! GOOD TO SEE YOU'RE ALIVE!
OH...

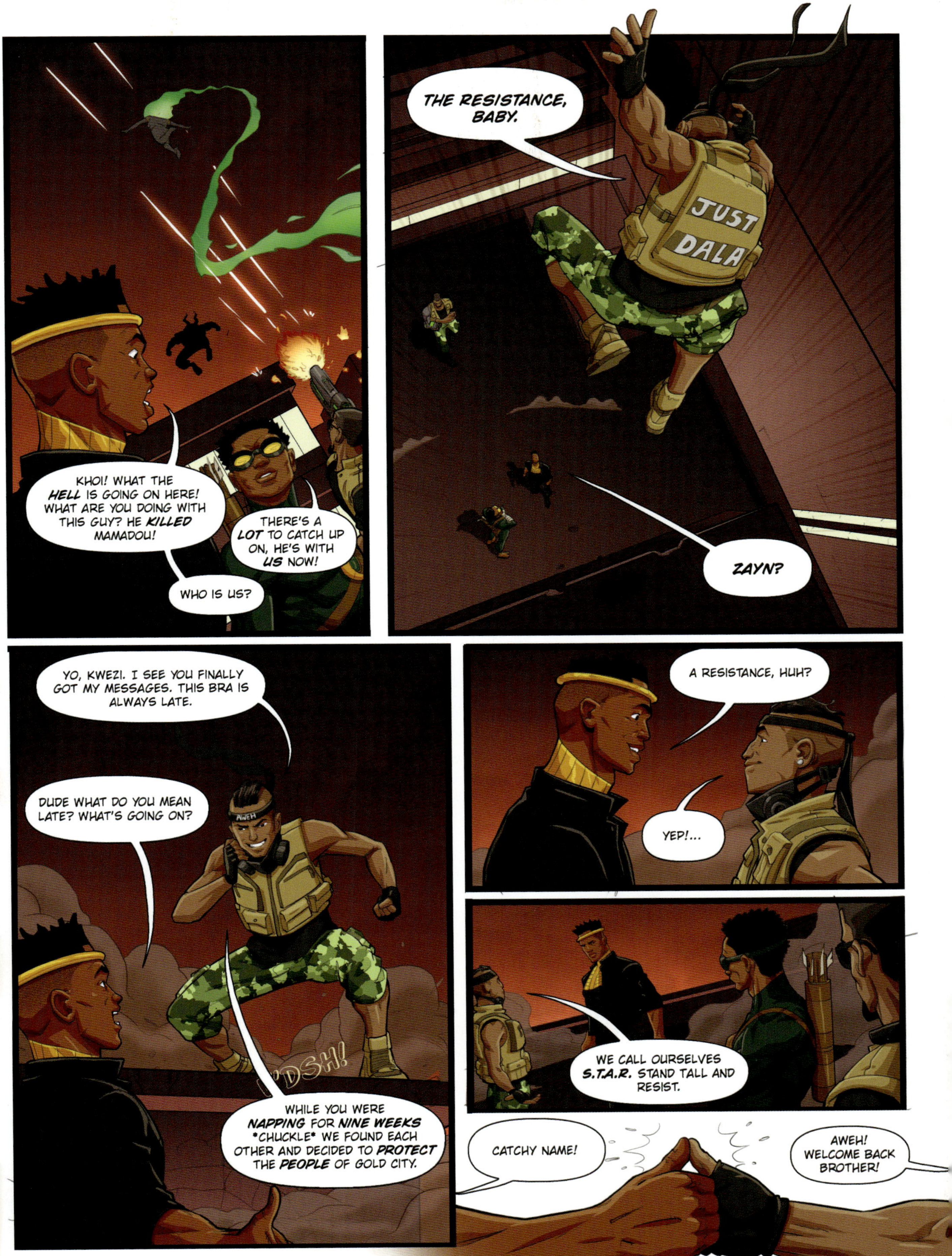
KHOI! WHAT THE HELL IS GOING ON HERE! WHAT ARE YOU DOING WITH THIS GUY? HE KILLED MAMADOU!
THERE'S A LOT TO CATCH UP ON, HE'S WITH US NOW!
WHO IS US?
THE RESISTANCE, BABY.
JUST DALA
ZAYN?
YO, KWEZI. I SEE YOU FINALLY GOT MY MESSAGES. THIS BRA IS ALWAYS LATE.
DUDE WHAT DO YOU MEAN LATE? WHAT'S GOING ON?
AWEH
WHILE YOU WERE NAPPING FOR NINE WEEKS *CHUCKLE* WE FOUND EACH OTHER AND DECIDED TO PROTECT THE PEOPLE OF GOLD CITY.
A RESISTANCE, HUH?
YEP!...
WE CALL OURSELVES S.T.A.R. STAND TALL AND RESIST.
CATCHY NAME!
AWEH! WELCOME BACK BROTHER!

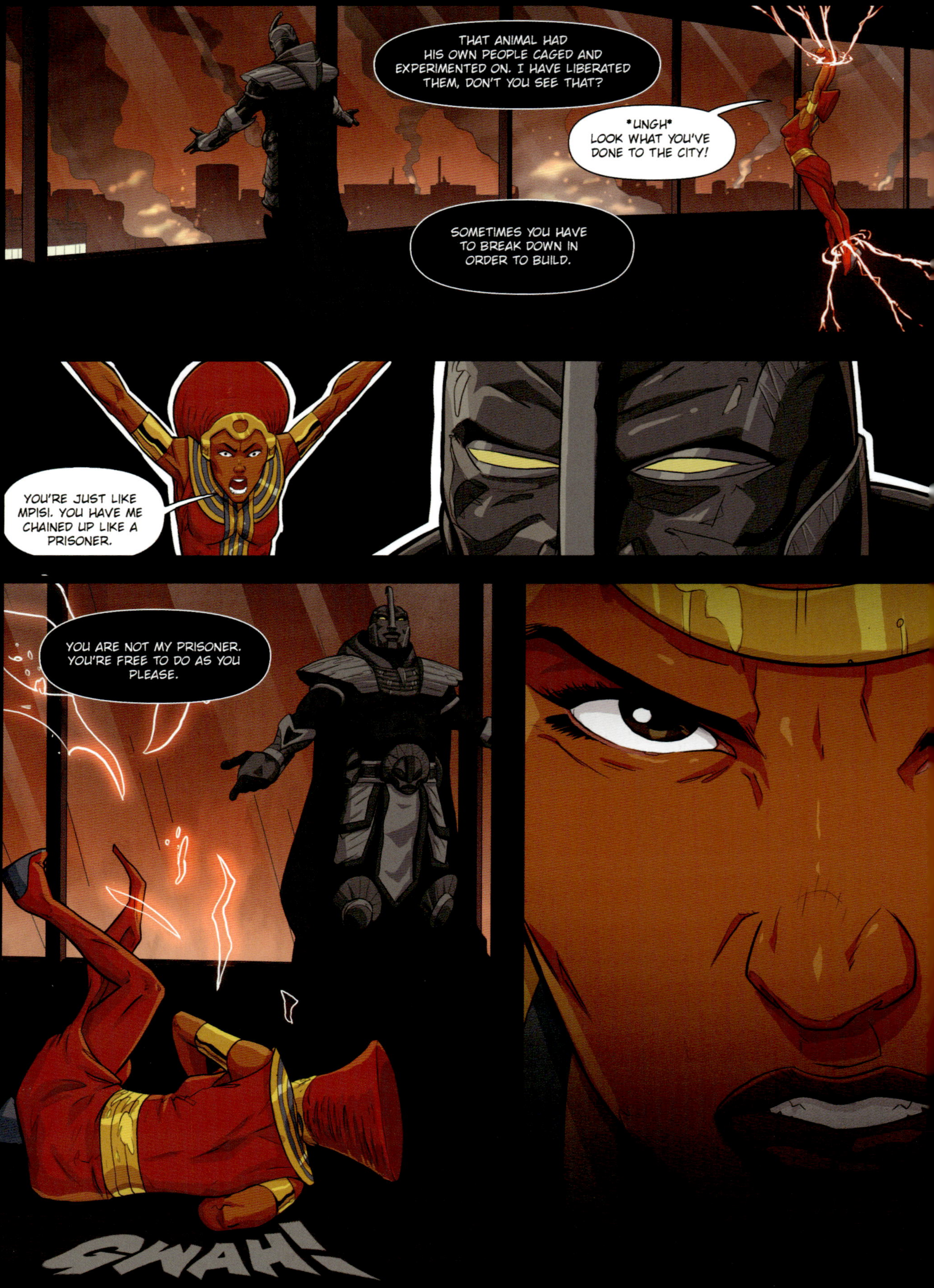
THAT ANIMAL HAD HIS OWN PEOPLE CAGED AND EXPERIMENTED ON. I HAVE LIBERATED THEM, DON'T YOU SEE THAT?
UNGH LOOK WHAT YOU'VE DONE TO THE CITY!
SOMETIMES YOU HAVE TO BREAK DOWN IN ORDER TO BUILD.
YOU'RE JUST LIKE MPISI. YOU HAVE ME CHAINED UP LIKE A PRISONER.
YOU ARE NOT MY PRISONER. YOU'RE FREE TO DO AS YOU PLEASE.
GNAH!

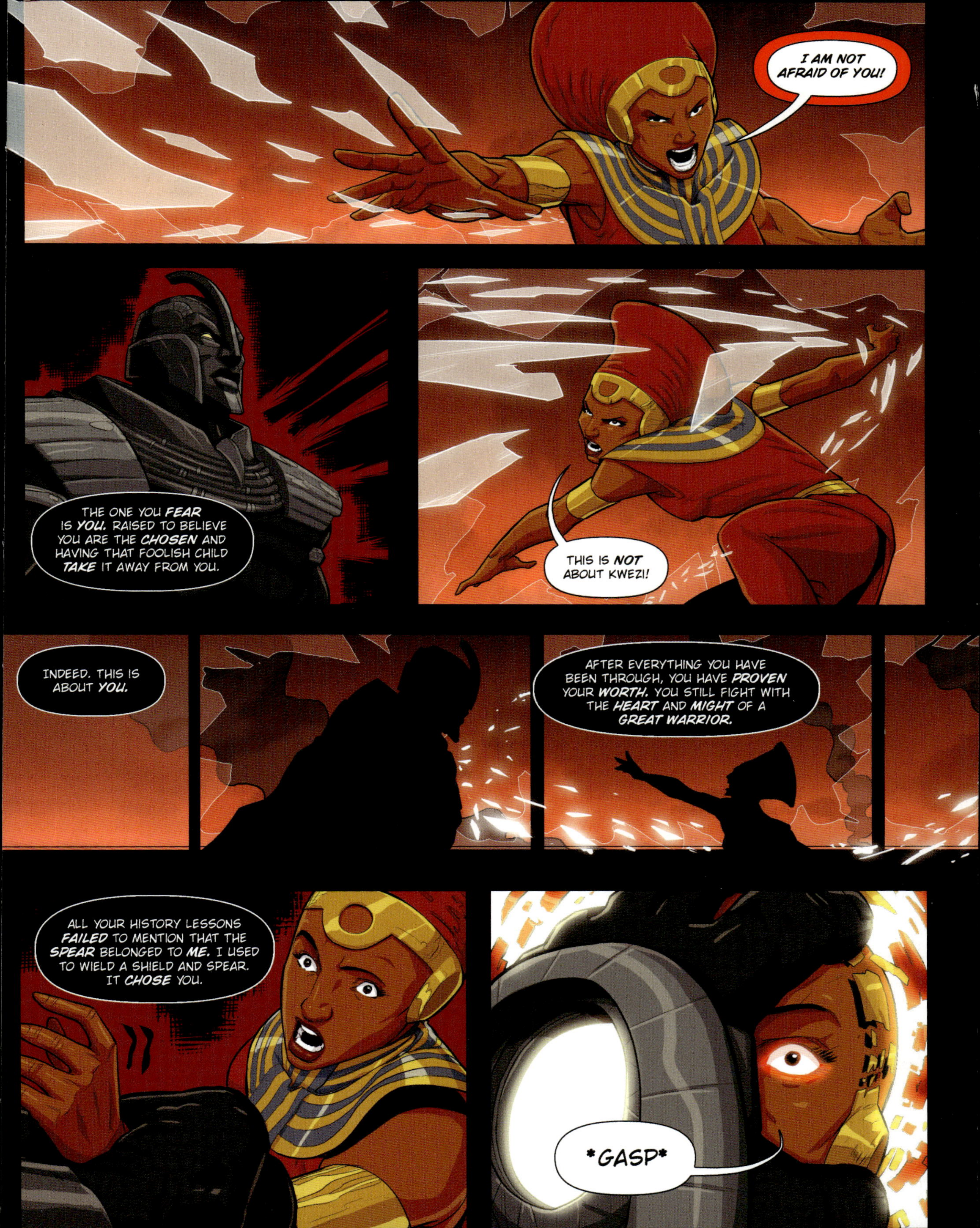
I AM NOT AFRAID OF YOU!
THE ONE YOU FEAR IS YOU. RAISED TO BELIEVE YOU ARE THE CHOSEN AND HAVING THAT FOOLISH CHILD TAKE IT AWAY FROM YOU.
THIS IS NOT ABOUT KWEZI!
INDEED. THIS IS ABOUT YOU.
AFTER EVERYTHING YOU HAVE BEEN THROUGH, YOU HAVE PROVEN YOUR WORTH. YOU STILL FIGHT WITH THE HEART AND MIGHT OF A GREAT WARRIOR.
ALL YOUR HISTORY LESSONS FAILED TO MENTION THAT THE SPEAR BELONGED TO ME. I USED TO WIELD A SHIELD AND SPEAR. IT CHOSE YOU.
GASP

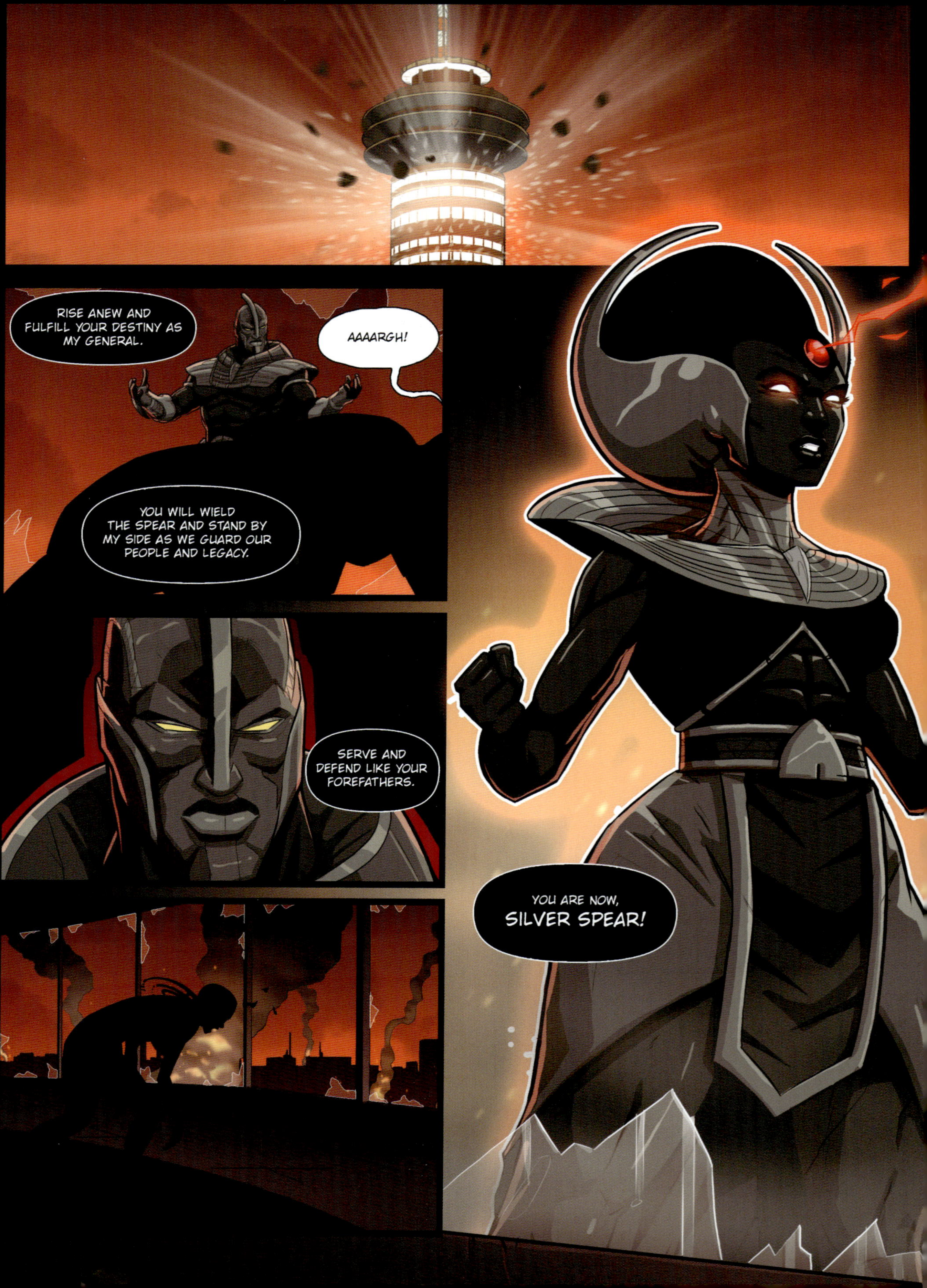
RISE ANEW AND FULFILL YOUR DESTINY AS MY GENERAL.
AAAARGH!
YOU WILL WIELD THE SPEAR AND STAND BY MY SIDE AS WE GUARD OUR PEOPLE AND LEGACY.
SERVE AND DEFEND LIKE YOUR FOREFATHERS.
YOU ARE NOW, SILVER SPEAR!

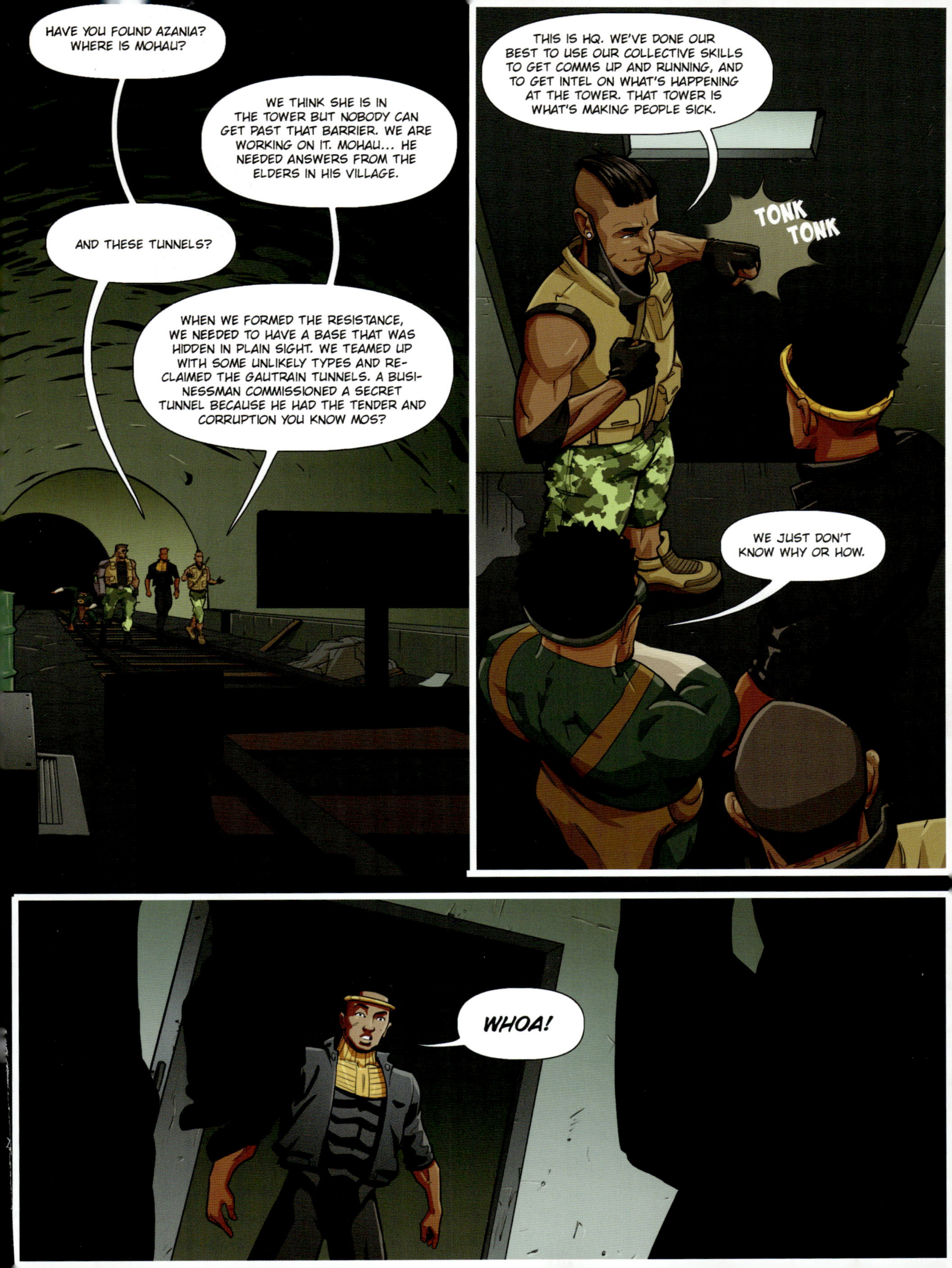
HAVE YOU FOUND AZANIA? WHERE IS MOHAU?
WE THINK SHE IS IN THE TOWER BUT NOBODY CAN GET PAST THAT BARRIER. WE ARE WORKING ON IT. MOHAU... HE NEEDED ANSWERS FROM THE ELDERS IN HIS VILLAGE.
AND THESE TUNNELS?
WHEN WE FORMED THE RESISTANCE, WE NEEDED TO HAVE A BASE THAT WAS HIDDEN IN PLAIN SIGHT. WE TEAMED UP WITH SOME UNLIKELY TYPES AND RE-CLAIMED THE GAUTRAIN TUNNELS. A BUSI-NESSMAN COMMISSIONED A SECRET TUNNEL BECAUSE HE HAD THE TENDER AND CORRUPTION YOU KNOW MOS?
THIS IS HQ. WE'VE DONE OUR BEST TO USE OUR COLLECTIVE SKILLS TO GET COMMS UP AND RUNNING, AND TO GET INTEL ON WHAT'S HAPPENING AT THE TOWER. THAT TOWER IS WHAT'S MAKING PEOPLE SICK.
TONK TONK
WE JUST DON'T KNOW WHY OR HOW.
WHOA!

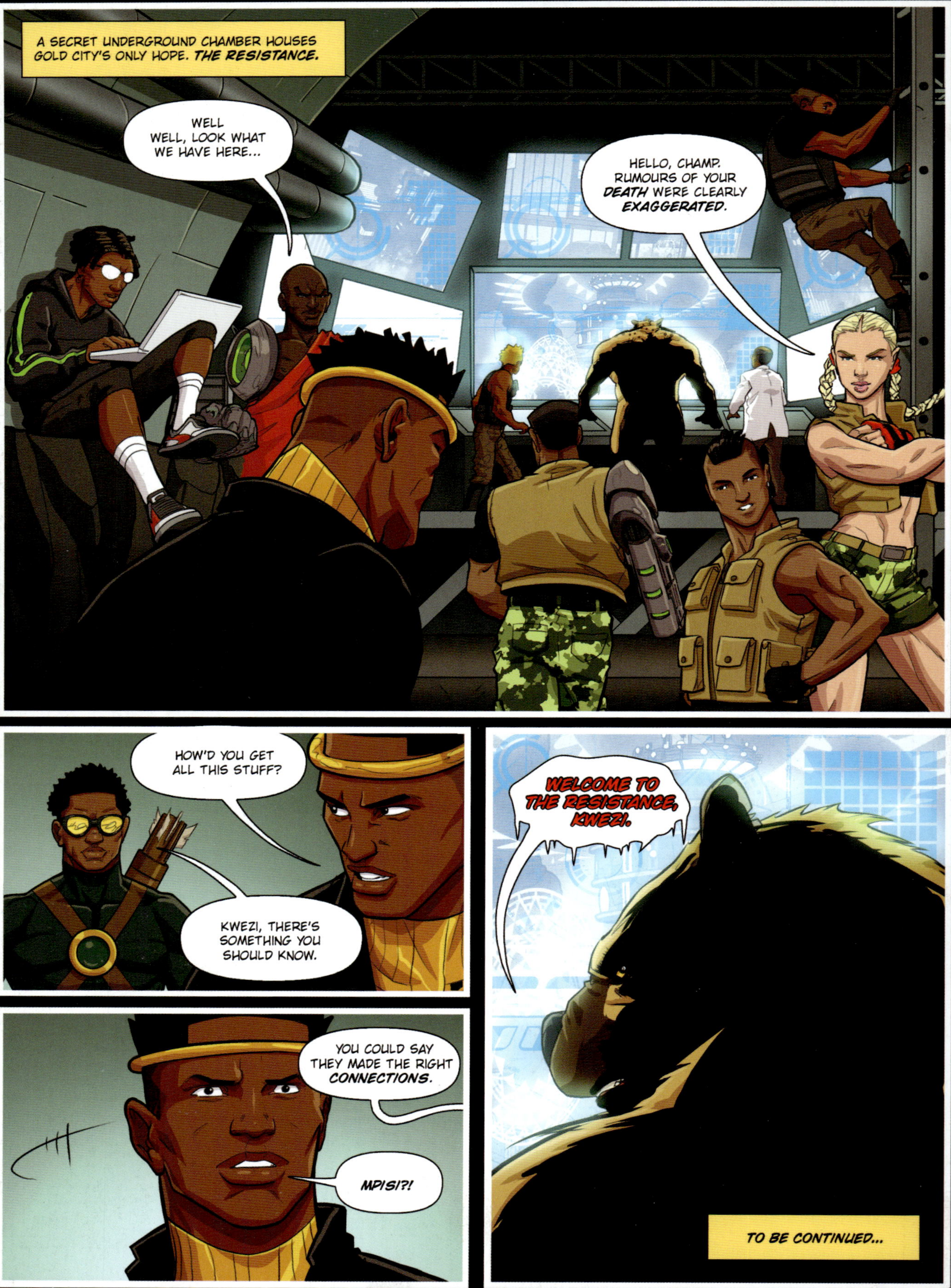
A SECRET UNDERGROUND CHAMBER HOUSES GOLD CITY'S ONLY HOPE. THE RESISTANCE.
WELL WELL, LOOK WHAT WE HAVE HERE...
HELLO, CHAMP. RUMOURS OF YOUR DEATH WERE CLEARLY EXAGGERATED.
HOW'D YOU GET ALL THIS STUFF?
KWEZI, THERE'S SOMETHING YOU SHOULD KNOW.
YOU COULD SAY THEY MADE THE RIGHT CONNECTIONS.
MPISI?!
WELCOME TO THE RESISTANCE, KWEZI.
TO BE CONTINUED...